A Beginner's Guide to the Study of Religion

A Beginner's Guide to the Study of Religion

Bradley L. Herling

continuum

Continuum International Publishing Group

The Tower Building
11 York Road
London SE1 7NX

80 Maiden Lane
Suite 704
New York NY 10038

www.continuumbooks.com

First published 2007

British Library Cataloguing-in-Publication Data
A catalogue record for this book is available from the British Library.

ISBN-10: PB: 0-8264-9531-1
ISBN-13: PB: 978-0-8264-9531-0

Library of Congress Cataloguing-in-Publication Data
A catalog record for this book is available from the Library of Congress.

Typeset by YHT Ltd, London
Printed and bound in Great Britain by Ashford Colour Press Ltd, Gosport, Hampshire

Contents

Preface for teachers and students

Beginnings

My own beginning with the academic study of religion goes back to my sophomore year in college. I still hadn't decided on a major and one night ducked into a lecture by Frederick Jameson. At the time I had no idea that Jameson was a prominent intellectual, and the content of his talk, though compelling, was a bit over my head. But the question/answer period generated a turning point for me. One of my friends bravely stood up and asked a question, which went something like this: "Prof. Jameson, you seem to be saying that even artists who are really *avant garde* are still just sell-outs. So my question is, if totally crazy, creative people can't change anything, then what about the rest of us? What are we supposed to do if we want to change the world we live in?"

Jameson paused for a moment and said, "Know everything." And that's pretty much where he left his answer.

Since then I have learned how to fit that answer into the broader context of Jameson's thought ("Always historicize," for those in the know), but when I heard it, this response struck me: it posed a challenge that only a young person could take literally. That semester I was taking my first classes in religion, and something clicked. Religion seemed to be everywhere, making its way into every facet of human history, so maybe studying *it* was the best way to "know everything." Soon after Jameson's lecture, I decided to become a religious-studies major.

You will be happy to know that I have gotten over the hubris inspired by Jameson's maxim. But my teachers in religious studies have consistently reinforced the *spirit* of that early insight. The study of religion spans the breadth of human experience, from one side of the globe to the other. It is also an exploration of one of the most powerful ways human beings discern *meaning, significance,* and *depth* in their world, as Jonathan Z. Smith has written:

What we study when we study religion is one mode of constructing worlds of meaning, worlds within which men find
themselves and in which they choose to dwell. What we study is
the passion and drama of man discovering the truth of what it is to
be human. History is the framework within whose perimeter those
human expressions, activities and intentionalities that we call
"religious" occur. Religion is the quest, within the bounds of the
human, historical condition, for the power to manipulate and
negotiate one's "situation" so as to have "space" in which to
meaningfully dwell. It is the power to relate one's domain to the
plurality of environmental and social spheres in such a way as to
guarantee the conviction that one's existence "matters". Religion
is a distinctive mode of human creativity, a creativity which both
discovers limits and creates limits for humane existence. What we
study when we study religion is the variety of attempts to map,
construct and inhabit such positions of power through the use of
myths, rituals and experiences of transformation.[1]

*Meaning, history, power, and creativity: religion is at a unique intersection
between these elements, taking shape in lived human experience.* As such, it
has made its way into most, if not all areas of our endeavor, and to that
extent, I had the right idea as an undergraduate, in my naïve way:
exploring religion affords us the opportunity to follow our curiosity in
any conceivable direction. It is in that spirit, one reaching back to my
own beginnings in the field, that I have written this book.

Literacy: Religious and theoretical

Truth be told, everyone who studies religion, even the "expert," has
to return to basics and wrestle with how to begin all the time. But this
book is designed for the student who is literally a beginner, just
getting underway in the field. Everyone is (or should be!) hungry for
information about religion these days, and it's out there, on shelf after
shelf at the local bookstore, or, better yet, in college and university
courses. In our complicated world, becoming *religiously literate* is a
great reason to get started with this subject matter.

In his recent best-selling book *Religious Literacy: What Every
American Needs to Know—And Doesn't*, Stephen Prothero makes a
convincing case for making this kind of start. Prothero shows that
education in religion, and thus knowledge about it, has deteriorated
dramatically in recent decades. It has gotten to the point that even
religious people do not know basic facts about their own tradition:
many Christians, for example, have a tough time naming the four

gospels, and about 10 per cent of American adults think that Noah's wife was Joan of Arc! Everyone needs to be religiously literate in our day and age, Prothero argues, because religion plays such a major role in global affairs, national politics, and everyday life.[2]

This argument is successful, but we should add to Prothero's plea: learning *how* to look at religion—becoming *theoretically* literate—is just as important as knowing *facts* about it. It's one thing to know the *content* of any given tradition. But what should we do with it? What does it mean? What does it mean for us now, we who are so hungry not only for information, but also for understanding?

Indeed, information only means something within a frame of reference, and everyone brings their own perspective to the interpretation of religious matters. But most people are not aware of the perspective they bring, and idiosyncratic interpretations often become facts, as if by magic. That's why we need to focus as much on the *how* as the *what* in the study of religion: studying theory and method makes us aware of our own perspective and leads to a more refined understanding—and the result is a religious literacy that goes deeper.

To address this challenge, preparation is necessary, and that is the purpose of this book: to get beginning students ready for learning *about* religion by presenting the most significant aspects of a *methodical* and *theoretical* approach to it. An informed intellectual approach helps the facts come through more clearly, but *theory and method also help us interpret and better understand what the facts might mean.*

As any teacher in the field will attest, introducing this layer is not an easy task: students often find it intimidating and abstract. As a response, this book is designed to make theory and method in the study of religion more accessible. The first step, taken in Chapter 1, is to establish the significance of studying religion now, in our historical present. Things we call religious are happening all around us, everyday, and they inevitably mean something to each of us, as individuals who are somehow wrapped up in them in our own lives, or simply as global citizens. As elements of self-understanding in studying religion, this first chapter incorporates some initial methodological steps: *self-consciousness, comparison, defamiliarization,* and *empathy.* Chapter 2 outlines the basic intellectual operations that we associate with taking a *theoretical, methodical* approach. As we take up the task of *interpreting* religion, we quickly begin to concern ourselves with *definition, description, explanation,* and *prediction.* With the right admixture of these operations, we have a better shot at bridging the divide between the world of the religious insider and the standpoint of the academic observer: we arrive at a better *understanding* of the challenging subject matter under study.

In the study of religion, this process is built on classic "theoretical ideas" that have been important in shaping the field. Chapters 3 and 4 contain a survey of some of the most significant of these ideas, and each chapter works along a distinct axis or spectrum of approaches. Chapter 3 charts a range of theories about *the fundamental experience of religion*, from the *individual* to the *social*, and contains accounts of Rudolf Otto, William James, Emile Durkheim, Max Weber, Victor Turner, and Clifford Geertz. Chapter 4 describes the theories of Karl Marx, Sigmund Freud, Carl Jung, Mircea Eliade, Ninian Smart, Paul Tillich, and Wilfred Cantwell Smith. Here the theories range from *critique* to *affirmation* of a religious essence. Finally, the concluding chapter highlights a set of pressing issues in the contemporary study of religion, which brings the survey of classic theories in the field up to date. Of course in a relatively short book like this, which is designed to accompany the already busy agenda of a college or university course, the contents are selective, and much has been left aside. And yet I am convinced that having read this guide, a beginning student (or general reader, for that matter), will be prepared for the "real stuff": the rich, complex subject matter that comes to us from religious worlds of meaning.

In my account, I have aimed for conciseness and clarity, without sacrificing thoroughness or complexity. The primary goal is to have students *do* something with theory and method when they confront the content of religion(s). This means that I often boil the ideas down to encourage application; each discussion of major theorists in the field, for example, is accompanied by a section entitled "What to look for," which briefly summarizes the main directives of any given approach. While the book does engage some of the complicated debates that concern scholars, I have emphasized comprehension of the foundations of these debates, rather than analyzing their intricate details or trying to resolve them. This approach leaves many questions open, questions that teachers and students will hopefully work on together. To add to this dialogue, I have often included quotes from the primary sources, which supplement the text and provide the basis for further discussion. Towards that end, this book also includes a list of selected resources to keep the student (and the autodidact) headed in the right direction.

One final note: while this text was primarily written for university and college students enrolled in religion courses, I hope that it will hold interest for "students" of religion in a broad sense: this book should provide resources for anyone who wants to think about how to approach this challenging phenomenon. It also represents the small beginning of a contribution to the discussion about the study of religion among my academic colleagues. I might condense my own perspective this way: for the sake of our students, our departments, our discipline, and for the sake of our world the way it is today, the academy needs to see "religion" as more than an "administrative title." We should consider allowing, for our students' sake at least, that there *are* very real "data" for the study of religion today. And we might note that the "construction" of religion by scholars is our (scholars') obsession; whatever *it* is that "religion" references is the world's. As informed observers for whom *it* has inevitably meant something (why disavow that?), we should prioritize our unique position as educators, emphasize the promotion of religious literacy and cross-cultural understanding—and thereby get on the side of our fellow global citizens, who so want and need to know more.

In the pages of this book, I try to express these sentiments as much to myself as I do to anyone else.

Notes

1 Jonathan Z. Smith, "Map Is Not Territory," in *Map Is Not Territory: Studies in the History of Religions* (Chicago and London: The University of Chicago Press, 1993), 290–91.

2 You are invited to take Prothero's religious literacy quiz. See www.deseretnews.com/dn/view/0,1249,660205799,00.html, or better yet, the version in the back of his book.

Acknowledgements

In the spirit of beginnings, I must recall and thank those who first introduced me to the study of religion at Wesleyan University, those who unknowingly abetted my quest to "know everything": Ron Cameron, Stephen Crites, Gene Klaaren, James Stone, Jan Willis, and Jeremy Zwelling. I also want to extend my deepest gratitude to those great mentors at Boston University who assisted me in making the transition from student to teacher—and from wild expectations to more focused (and sustainable) ones: John Clayton, Paula Fredriksen, Ray Hart, Robert Neville, and Alan Olson. David Eckel deserves special mention and thanks: his ubiquitous "toolbox" for the study of religion served as an inspiration for this book, as did (more importantly) his elegant and insightful approach to teaching religion.

This book had its origins in the content I produced for the "Why Study Religion" website sponsored by the American Academy of Religion. For their inspiration and guidance in getting that project off the ground (and therefore this one as well), I wish to acknowledge both Warren Frisina and Carey Gifford. While traces of the original website remain, this book moves forward in terms of detail and scope. For giving me the continuing opportunity to work with these ideas, I thank Continuum, and particularly my editor, Rebecca Vaughan-Williams, for her encouragement and extreme patience. I must also recognize a set of colleagues who took the time to offer feedback on this project in its early stages: Kristi Swenson, Elijah Siegler, Kelly Pemberton, Patricia Lennon, Corinne Dempsey, Tim Vivian, David Frankfurter, and Richard Pilgrim. Thanks also to Martyn Oliver and Shawn Gorman for their valuable feedback on the text along the way, and a special "shout out" to Gene Gallagher for coming through in a pinch with a fantastic set of responses. Of course, despite all of this help, any flaws in the final product should be attributed to me alone. Finally, I also thank my wife, Maria, who keeps me on the ground (most of the time).

The word about the "Why Study Religion" website came to me from Barbara DeConcini, the former Executive Director of the

American Academy of Religion, and it represented yet one more door that Barbara has opened for me intellectually and professionally. The most pivotal chapter in my own education in the study of religion occurred during my time as the administrative assistant for the AAR from 1992 to 1994. I often say that I got my Master's in the study of religion from the AAR—and Barbara was my advisor. Since then, she has been an unflagging supporter and insightful mentor, and this book certainly would never have been written without her influence.

I would like to dedicate this text to Barbara DeConcini, in recognition of her stewardship of the field as a whole over the 15 years she served as Executive Director of the AAR, and, personally, out of heartfelt gratitude for her support and friendship over the years.

1 Beginnings in the study of religion

Over the last two hundred years, predictions that religion would soon disappear have been common. In the nineteenth century, for example, philosopher Friedrich Nietzsche declared God dead—and even proposed that we ourselves had killed him. Soon thereafter sociologists began to announce the inevitability of secularization, the process by which religion loses its influence over society and individuals. And later, Sigmund Freud proposed that religious belief was a collective delusion that humanity would imminently outgrow. Even today, scientists and philosophers claim to be on the verge of "breaking the spell" by arguing that religious consciousness evolved as a survival technique that is no longer necessary. So we have to ask: is religion on the way out, and, if so, why should we continue to study it?

Observing today's world, it seems that rumors of religion's demise have been seriously exaggerated. For now (and for the foreseeable future) it is here to stay, perhaps because it is much more complicated than its critics have suspected. Religion continues to be intertwined with human life: we find it at the center of global issues, cultural conflict, and political debate; on television, in film, in popular music; surrounding us in our cities, towns, and neighborhoods; in the lives of the people we know and love; and (for some of us) in ourselves, as we live out and wrestle with our own beliefs and customs. *Despite those who have predicted and perhaps hoped for its disappearance, religion keeps showing up, calling out for examination, not as something that is dead or dying, but as a vivid, thriving phenomenon—something that, at the very least, we must live with.*

If you are reading this book, then you are probably somehow drawn to this phenomenon and want to know more about it. Perhaps you are preparing to study it in a class, or maybe you are exploring the topic on your own. In either case, before delving into the content, it is necessary to think about how to approach it. What do you already know about religion, where should you be coming from as you begin to study it, and why is it important to study religion right now? This chapter will invite reflection on these questions, and along the way you will learn some first steps in religious studies *method*, steps that begin to bring your object of study into focus.

Skepticism about religion

"Whither is God? . . . I will tell you. *We have killed him*—you and I. All of us are his murderers. But how did we do this? . . . Gods, too, decompose. God is dead. God remains dead. And we have killed him."[1]

Friedrich Nietzsche

"In short not only is the sphere of religion not increasing . . . but it is continually diminishing. This regression did not begin at any precise moment in history, but one can follow the phases of its development from the very origins of social evolution."[2]

Emile Durkheim

"Religion would thus be the universal obsessional neurosis of humanity . . . If this view is right, it is to be supposed that a turning-away from religion is bound to occur with the fatal inevitability of a process of growth, and that we find ourselves at this very juncture . . . "[3]

Sigmund Freud

"The spell that I say *must* be broken is the taboo against a forthright, scientific, no-holds-barred investigation of religion as one natural phenomenon among many."[4]

Daniel C. Dennett

"I want to know how other people live"

When students are asked about why they take religion classes, many respond with statements like the following:

"I want to understand people."
"I want to know why religious people do the things they do."
"I want to know about other cultures."
"I want to know what makes people tick."

And finally, here's one that seems to encapsulate all the rest:

"I want to know how other people live."

These responses capture the baseline curiosity that drives this area of inquiry. Why study religion now? Because, as Alice in Wonderland said, how other people live keeps getting "curioser and curioser."

In contemplating your own interest, step back for a moment and allow your imagination to range. What do you already know about religion? What examples do you associate with this concept? Where does it seem to be *happening* right now in our world, as you read these words?

Write down your own examples, and then consider these:

If it's the right time of the year, along one of the dusty highways of northern India a young man wearing an orange t-shirt and matching gym shorts is lying down for a rest in a tent. His shirt features an iron-on image of Shiva, one of the most powerful and respected gods in the Hindu tradition. The young man has been walking for five straight days in the blistering heat; he has been sleeping in makeshift camps erected by the side of the road. Why is he doing this? He glances over at what is next to him: an elaborately festooned three-foot long pole (called a *kanwar*) with two jugs of water hanging from either end, suspended above the ground by a pair of sawhorses. He has been shouldering this burden for over a hundred miles, always keeping it off the ground, and now he is halfway home to his small village in the Indian countryside. There he first made a vow to his god, his family, and his community months ago: to go to the holy Ganges river (Shiva's river) and retrieve its water for the purification of the village shrine. The young man believes this deed will bring him favor with the god in this life and good karma in preparation for the next.

Meanwhile, on a beautiful Greek island in the middle of the Aegean, a young woman is contemplating the task she has set for herself. At the top of a steep hill, about half a mile away, a large Orthodox church that houses a miraculous icon awaits her. She thinks about her younger brother dying of cancer in Athens and prepares to crawl up to the church on the cobblestones as thousands have done before her. She opts not to wear knee-pads, like others have, nor does she wrap her knees to keep them from bleeding. No, she will crawl with her knees bare, because if she can sacrifice herself to show her devotion to the mother of Christ, who himself died to release humanity from its suffering, she will be able to intercede on behalf of her brother. And perhaps she will be able to save him.

Now, in Seattle, all the preparations are in place: the DJ, the food, the decorations. It will be a great party. All the relatives are in town, and everyone is having a good time the day before, except for one 12-year-old girl. She is nervous because she just *knows* that she will "mess up" her Torah portion, the passage from the Bible that she has to read in front of everyone at her Bat Mitzvah—or, as her rabbi told her, when she *becomes* a Bat Mitzvah (a daughter of the commandments).

She has been practicing intensively, and the rabbi has been very nice, teaching her about why the ritual is so important to being Jewish and giving her his ideas about God's mysterious but persistent care for his people. Despite all that, she is still *really* nervous, though trying not to show it.

At the same time, a man arrives in an airport as he travels on business from Pakistan. He is neatly but casually dressed in Western-style clothes, and he keeps his briefcase close at hand. His arrival is a little late, and now he is in a rush because the alarm in his watch is going off. This watch is special: not only does it tell the time, but it also reminds the Muslim wearer when to pray and what direction to face when doing so. The man hurries to the nearest bathroom and washes his hands and face quickly in the proscribed way (no time for the feet!). Then he rushes to the ecumenical chapel, where he arrives just in time. It is time to kneel down, to submit to Allah, as he does dutifully five times a day. Now what about a prayer mat? Seeing nothing available, the man takes the morning edition of *The Financial Times* from under his arm and spreads the newspaper on the floor in a corner. He consults his watch, faces Mecca (somewhere off to the southeast), kneels down on the newspaper, and begins the prayer cycle. Sometimes travelers must make do, and God understands that.

Moving to a second floor studio in one of the bustling neighborhoods of Tokyo, people from all walks of life are sitting in a circle, all of them cross-legged, some in full lotus position. Apart from the occasional noise from the street below, the room is very, very quiet because the people are just sitting, just breathing. Their minds are full of thoughts that race back and forth, but, as the Buddha taught, they allow a thought to happen, say to themselves, "That's a thought!" and then gently try to bring their focus back to just breathing, just sitting. They do not fill their minds with a god, with a saint, or with a feeling: in fact, they want to empty themselves, because the Buddha taught that relief from suffering comes from realizing that there is no self.

And now (depending once more on what time of the year it is), maybe there's a baseball game happening in Boston's Fenway Park. During the seventh inning stretch, the crowd sings "God Bless America." In the top of the seventh, one of the best players on the visiting team made the last out, despite having done everything according to his routine, a long and elaborate set of hand gestures that get him ready to hit before every pitch. To some observers, they look like a ritual, some kind of obsessive or magical incantation. But he failed to get a hit. Now, in the bottom of the inning, the slugger for the home team approaches the plate. He has no elaborate pre-hitting ritual. He just waits for the pitch, swings, and sends the ball high into the upper deck. But as he crosses home plate, he points to the sky, looks up, and says, "For you." The crowd roars.

In some other part of the world, or maybe not so far away, another one of our fellow human beings thinks about his enemies with disdain, as symbols of the world's corruption. He thinks, "Would a strike against all of these faithless enemies not bring happiness to the divine? Would it not earn the agent of divine will a place of honor in this life and beyond?" The true religion for this devotee is a religion of the original word—and of anger and vengeance. "So much has been done to stamp us out," he says to himself, "but the true warriors continue to stand up and fight. And the sacrifice continues . . ." What's strange about this imagining is that the source and location of the voice is not clear: is it Muslim, Christian, Jewish, Hindu, or something else?

And so it goes, on and on, countless instances of religious happenings here and there, right now. After reading these examples, what stories would you tell as you continue to reflect on what you already know?

Just by considering these examples, and your own, your study is underway: telling your stories is a way of getting your associations and assumptions on the table. In consulting your experiences and then expressing them, you are also engaging in description, which is an important research skill. And further, you are thinking about that key question: why should I study religion right now? Here we have one firm answer: *religion is not just a vague abstraction or media phenomenon but is instead an active and real force in day-to-day existence for many of our fellow human beings.* You are right to be curious about it, perhaps because you want to become an informed global citizen, or maybe you are simply driven by the curiosity itself—because it is good to know about how other people live.

Studying religion means something . . . to you

The study of religion is not just about why someone out there, off in some (sort of) distant place, does what he or she does. It is also about us, about those of us who decide to examine this phenomenon. Sometimes the quest can be quite personal: it is not unusual to find Hindus in classes on Hinduism, Jews studying Judaism, Christians enrolled in classes on the New Testament, and so on. People are often interested because they want to learn more about their own tradition, especially in comparison with others.

This is a fine rationale that is most often welcomed in the religious studies classroom, but *one does not need to be religious or come from a religious background to study religion.* In an academic setting, the investigation of religion promotes *understanding* of both oneself and others: it is relevant for everyone. As is the case with humanities disciplines like literature or philosophy, the deepest issues are often at stake. What is the most important thing in life? What is the right way to live? What is the meaning of life and death? Is there something beyond this world? Are there higher powers that stand outside our world and also direct it? Are we free to choose our fate, or has it been predetermined? What is most true and reliable: the products of our mind? Our feelings? A text? An experience? Why is there suffering in the world, and can we do anything about it? And so on. Religions are distinctive, however, because within them these questions often become a *lived reality.* Religious people tend to *live out* their responses to profound questions rather than just reading or talking about them, and so, by observing and listening to these individuals, and by studying their traditions, beliefs, and practices, we gain insight into *our own* responses to the challenging questions that confront every human being.

Four important principles in religious-studies *method* can guide you in thinking about the study of religion as a project in interpreting not only what's "out there," but also in understanding yourself: *self-consciousness, comparison, defamiliarization,* and *empathy.*

Self-consciousness

It's safe to assume that religion means *something* to everyone because everyone has experience with it. Some of us come from religious traditions. Others do not or have moved away from their background. But all of us have preconceived notions going in: this generic term "religion" that we keep throwing around elicits some association and response. When we try to understand anything, especially when it comes to something that seems to have such significance, it is necessary to get clear on where we stand as observers from the outset. Every beginning student comes with "baggage," so identifying your own history (and the views it has produced) will enhance your objectivity and openness as you proceed.

At this point, pause in your reading once again. Where *are* you coming from? Do you have a religious background, or not? What expectations about religion do you have? What do you think about religion in general, or about religious expressions that are different from your own? How might your own experience color the way you look at other people?

These are difficult questions, requiring long and thoughtful answers, but we can bring them into focus by imagining that you are about to have a conversation with the following "types":

- A skeptical atheist, the son or daughter of two scientists.
- An evangelical Christian who believes that the Bible is the literal word of God.
- A "New Age" child of "hippies" who believes in spirituality but not organized religion.
- A Jewish student who observes on Yom Kippur and Passover, but generally doesn't go to synagogue.
- A black belt in karate who has begun to subscribe to the tenets of Zen Buddhism.
- The child of a mixed marriage between a lapsed Catholic and a self-proclaimed "cultural Jew."
- A student from a generally Christian/Protestant background whose family never really took going to church or religion seriously.
- Someone who grew up in a Catholic family, went to Catholic school and, while remaining Catholic, is somewhat ambivalent about that whole experience.
- A nature lover who gets into the outdoors as much as he can because of its intense beauty and calming serenity.
- A Hindu who is used to having an altar devoted to several gods in his family home, but he believes that all religions are essentially teaching the same message.
- A Muslim committed to following the will of Allah: she can't understand Christianity with its Trinity and three gods in one.

Obviously these examples are selective and simplified, but we can use them to imagine just how much a person's background might affect the way he or she views any given religious phenomenon. What will the committed monotheist think when encountering people worshiping in a polytheistic tradition—and *vice versa*? Will a literalist from one tradition have a hard time seeing the merits of another's scriptures? What does a committed atheist bring to the table, and what about someone whose experience with religion has been, at best, ambivalent? What about those who are only mildly religious, who, in their own lives, prefer that it doesn't interfere too much? Of course, the questions can go on and on, but they indicate one inevitable truth: it is crucial to acknowledge biases at the beginning of our attempt to understand the worldview of others.

There are different schools of thought about what to do with background assumptions once they have been highlighted. *A phenomenological approach, for example, urges us to "bracket" assumptions so our object of study can appear as it is, without any filters.* So if a Protestant Christian wants to study religion, she must set aside her prior beliefs and assumptions about what religion is, and only then can she observe other traditions as they really are. For example, if a Protestant observer goes looking for a Bible in each tradition she encounters (because that is such a focal point in her own worldview), she will often be frustrated or misled. What is the "Bible" of Shintoism, or of an Australian aboriginal tradition? Are the scriptures within Buddhism or Hinduism like the Bible in the Christian tradition? Despite its value in challenging our biases, however, this approach always provokes debate. Is it possible to be *completely* objective, to leave all of our "baggage" behind, even if we try our best to do so?

Another approach is *hermeneutical: understanding gets started when we put our prior judgments and assumptions out there and then test them against what we observe.* In this case, instead of bracketing our own background assumptions, we allow them to come to the forefront as the starting point for our investigation. So the Protestant Christian asks "Protestant Christian questions" about other traditions and realizes that some fit and many do not: then she adjusts her expectations in order to achieve a more authentic interpretation. So the Bible may be the only place to start in asking questions about the role of scripture (or lack thereof) within non-Christian religions for some observers. But the key to the hermeneutical method is remaining open to adjustments when what we encounter challenges our prior assumptions.

These two approaches are distinctive, but there is also common ground between them. The *phenomenological* approach recommends taking a step away from our background assumptions in order to let religious phenomena shine through, while the *hermeneutical* approach proposes that understanding only happens when we are willing to put prior judgments into play. Despite this difference in emphasis, in both cases we are urged to be methodologically *self-conscious* when studying religion, to identify our own background and biases, so they do not distort the process of interpretation without our awareness. This procedure improves our perception of the religious worldviews of others, but it also, by necessity, teaches us about ourselves.

Comparison

Comparison is a vital analytical tool that builds from methodological self-consciousness. Max Müller, a prominent nineteenth-century scholar, established one of the most basic principles in the study of religion: *"He who knows one, knows none."*[5] Understanding moves forward, Müller argued, with comparisons and contrasts that are measured

"The term *epoche* ... implies that no judgment is expressed concerning the objective world, which is thus placed 'between brackets', as it were. All phenomena, therefore, are considered solely as they are presented to the mind, without any further aspects such as their real existence, or their value, being taken into account; in this way the observer restricts himself to pure description systematically pursued, himself adopting the attitude of complete intellectual suspense, or of abstention from all judgment, regarding these controversial topics."[6]

Gerardus van der Leeuw

"The essence of the *question* is to open up possibilities and keep them open. If a prejudice [a prior judgment about something we interpret] becomes questionable in view of what another person or text says to us, this does not mean that it is simply set aside and the text or the other person accepted as valid in its place ... In fact our own prejudice is properly brought into play by being put at risk. Only by being given full play is it able to experience the other's claim to truth and make it possible for him to have full play himself."[7]

Hans-Georg Gadamer

even-handedly, and he had a point. If we want to appreciate what makes one form of music unique, for example, we have to compare it with others. If we wish to evaluate current events (say, for example, the American involvement in Iraq), then we compare it with previous episodes (like the Vietnam War) to see what can be learned. Comparison is an indispensable tool for identifying, clarifying, and ultimately understanding any given phenomenon.

"The process of comparison is a fundamental characteristic of human intelligence ... comparison, the bringing together of two or more objects for the purpose of noting either similarity or dissimilarity, is the omnipresent substructure of human thought. Without it, we could not speak, perceive, learn, or reason ... That comparison has, at times, led us astray there can be no doubt; that comparison remains *the* method of scholarship is likewise beyond question."[8]

Jonathan Z. Smith

So, in order to gain insight into *religious* phenomena, Müller argued, we must compare, and even if we are firmly grounded in our own religious tradition, its meaning is not *truly* known without comparative study. You will notice that this principle can take two different directions: one leads towards understanding the religious world *out there*, and the other leads to *self*-understanding. In keeping with the first impulse, many scholars have pursued the comparative study of religion with an eye towards both broad patterns and fruitful contrasts. Is it possible that there are common, archetypal patterns that manifest themselves in many, or *all* religions? Only by collecting data and making comparisons is there any hope of making that case. What makes a particular religious practice, or an entire tradition, unique? Contrasting it with others leads to answers. On both fronts, whether we emphasize similarity or difference in the study of religion, comparative analysis is a powerful tool for discerning the significance of what we observe in the world "out there."

But for Müller, comparison was also a necessary component of self-understanding. He went so far as to say that the practitioner of a given religious tradition fails to understand it if he or she does not study others. In order to grasp this part of the comparative principle, recall that old maxim: "Ignorance is bliss." It is tempting to enclose oneself within a worldview, refusing exposure to any others, so as to avoid challenges, and that goes for religious and non-religious perspectives alike. Absent comparison, contrast, and perspective, our knowledge of one worldview is incomplete: it's like tasting one flavor of ice cream (or perhaps tasting it over and over again and knowing it very well and also being completely in love with it) and then proclaiming that we know what flavored ice cream is all about. Pushing Müller's idea further, adherence to one worldview, without comparative analysis, may even be an ignorant and empty gesture. How can we know that our way of life is best without vigorous comparison with other possibilities? And without that comparative analysis, how can we consider our adherence to one worldview genuine and authentic?

At the very least, comparison accompanies methodological self-consciousness as a vital part of our attempt to understand religion. By saying that one thing is similar to or the same as something else, and by saying that things are different from each other, we begin to establish the significance of what the world presents to us.

Defamiliarization

A principle that extends on comparison in religious studies is called *defamiliarization*: "making the familiar seem strange *in order to enhance our perception of the familiar.*"[9] Defamiliarization also has an inverse: at the same time, make the strange seem familiar. How does this two-sided operation work?

To bring the first part of the idea into focus, just think about the movies. In so many films, the premise is rendering the familiar strange, which produces a challenge to our usual perception of things. In *The Matrix*, for example, the world is an illusion constructed by evil machines whose agents are everywhere. In this case, the film compels us to see our usual experience and beliefs not only from the outside but also in a radically new light. After seeing it for the first time, did you wonder just for a moment about whether the world of your senses was "really there"? If so, that's defamiliarization, and its effect was to make you question what is "really real." (If you haven't seen *The Matrix*, you can probably think of many other examples that produce this same effect.)

In applying this principle to the study of religion, it should be noted that defamiliarization does not entail attacking religious traditions by making them seem "weird." Instead, we merely want "to enhance our perception of the familiar" by shaking things up a bit, leading to new insights.

Many people are familiar, for example, with the Bible as a "book," a unified product of divine revelation. Fair enough. From the very beginning, however, we have to be open to something strange: the Bible seems to contain *different* voices, as if a number of different stories and texts were stitched together by an editor of some kind. Discerning these different voices *defamiliarizes* the text and forces us to think hard about what the Bible, scripture, and revelation are all about in religious traditions.

Another Biblical instance: the dichotomy between the wrathful God of the Hebrew Bible and the loving God of the New Testament is familiar to many, and perhaps there's something to it. But to defamiliarize this characterization and "enhance our perception" of it, we must register the strange moments where Jesus (sometimes without warning) seems to fly off the handle.[10] Now we must inquire further about the concept of divine love in the early Christian tradition and how it overlaps with the role of prophets and the messiah from the Jewish tradition; now the familiar contrast is not so cut and dried.

And a final example, now thinking about the present day: for many, "normal," everyday, relatively non-religious American life is what's familiar. But what if we identified a set of civic rituals that many of us as citizens perform, rituals that seem to offer "a genuine apprehension of universal and transcendent religious reality ... as revealed through the experience of the American people"—singing "God Bless America" at a baseball game, for example?[11] That would defamiliarize the "secular," leading to deeper reflection on the distinction between it and "the religious." Perhaps the secular goes under the guise of being irreligious, but it also contains traces of religious forms of life that still serve as its basis.

In sum, the study of religion is full of surprises: defamiliarization is the principle that keeps us as students open to what they have to teach us. Surprises provoke thought and reflection, and that is what the study of religion is all about.

Empathy

The inverse of defamiliarization calls for openness to surprises that run in the opposite direction: we should be ready for cases where what seems at first to be strange becomes familiar, leading to an intellectual connection with it. Then it is possible to pursue a powerful act of understanding within the study of religion: *empathy*. Once we familiarize ourselves with a foreign worldview, it is most fully understood when we imagine what it would be like to take it on, "to walk a mile in someone else's moccasins," as prominent scholar of religion Ninian Smart was fond of saying.

Once again, movies can help us understand this principle. Films regularly prompt us to find something recognizable in a character we would usually find strange, or even horrifying. A shocking example appears in the movie *Monster*, in which Charlize Theron plays a prostitute who becomes a serial killer. Her lifestyle, character, and deeds are beyond "strange": they are repellent. And yet the film suggests that this character commits her crimes out of an outrage about her own victimization and a passionate (but misguided) loyalty to her companion. To this extent, her motivations are familiar, and, as a consequence, we feel a sense of commonality, even with this rather scary person. But the film takes one step further: it builds on our connection with her and often gets us to see things from her point of view. That's different from simply recognizing something familiar. Now that recognition has become empathy, and we begin to "familiarize" ourselves with her worldview, we can understand where she's coming from, even though she is a "monster."

In the study of religion, these steps can be extremely valuable. When we examine a tradition that is foreign and perhaps "strange," finding a familiarity begins the dialogue. If Theravada Buddhism is very *un*familiar to you, for example, then the Buddha's proclamations that express the value of self-reliance and common sense might provide a good starting point. Or if Islam is strange to you, and you come from a Christian or Jewish background, then recognizing its deep commitment to monotheism may be a key to unlocking it. But making the strange familiar is not *just* about looking for familiarities.

What we recognize as familiar in the other tradition is only the gateway to becoming *so* familiar with that worldview that it is possible to take it up in our *empathetic imagination*. So here is the real challenge: if Theravada Buddhism is foreign to you, how would you look at the world if you were Buddhist layperson living in Sri Lanka? If Islam is unfamiliar to you, can you imagine what it would be like to be a Muslim walking the streets of Jakarta? With enough openness and familiarization, you can perform operations like these, which will lead you to a new, more in-depth understanding.

But not only that: empathy, or seeing the world through the eyes of another, is a vital aspect of *self*-education; it is yet another way that studying religion comes to mean something . . . to you.

Religion on the global and national stage

This chapter got off the ground with a vital question: why study religion right now? First we brought to mind that religion calls out for attention because it is yet a living, lived reality for so many of our fellow human beings. Then it became clear that this area of inquiry also has meaning for you, the student. If reliable methodological principles guide us, our investigation leads to a better interpretation of religion "out there," but it also promotes self-understanding.

To bring home the urgency of studying religion *now*, however, we must think in *historical* terms. Most would associate "history" with inquiring into the past, and that is certainly correct. But to be precise, historical consciousness means inquiring into the past *in light of present concerns* and *thinking of ourselves as living history now under circumstances that the past has produced*. The "history of religions," taken as the recovery of religious phenomena from the past, has its own integrity and interest, but what is pressing about the study of religions, and particularly how they have developed and arrived where they are *now*, is our current situation. And many would argue that given our *current historical situation*, the study of religion has *never* been more important.

The global situation
Many of us will most readily associate religion, and the need to study it, with its significant role in the grand cultural and political conflicts that grip our world today. According to The Pew Forum on Religion and Public Life, in 2005 75 per cent of Americans reported that religion has "a great deal" or "a fair amount" to do with these conflicts. If we hope to discern the significance of examining religion

in our current historical situation, then this seems to be a good place to start.

Religion interacts with modern political institutions to produce conflict in many different forms.[12] On some occasions religious factions attempt to take over a nation, causing conflict between secularists and religionists. Iran is a good example of a nation where this takeover happened, and in its wake, the secularists were killed or exiled, along with the members of the non-dominant religious faction. In other situations, the nation is not taken over entirely, but a majority faction sets the terms of culture and politics, and often internal strife with rival groups is the result. India is not a religious state, and it is a democracy, and yet Hinduism is the dominant and most influential worldview there, which often leads to tensions with the most significant minority religious group, the Muslims. The next type of conflict involves the split of a nation into rival religious factions that have their own territory and often end up fighting a civil war with each other. For years Protestants and Catholics fought this kind of battle in Northern Ireland, such a conflict persists in Sri Lanka where Hindus and (surprisingly enough) Buddhists square off against each other, and religion certainly plays an important role in the continuing struggle between Israelis and Palestinians. Finally, we are familiar with situations where the "nation" totally falls apart along religious lines: this happened, to a certain extent, in the former Yugoslavia, and we witness it again today in Iraq. Overall, these forms of religious conflict, and the many other examples that go with them, really make us wonder. Is religion a force for good, or does it only promote tension, division, and violence? What has happened within various religions that has *radicalized* some of their members enough to commit violence? How does religion intersect with culture and politics such that conflict and war take on a religious character? Can religion ever be an *antidote* to violence?

These questions are all the more vivid when we think about one of the major challenges of our current historical situation: religious terrorism. Contemporary terrorism represents a way in which religious conflict and violence *transcend* the boundaries of the nation. Some Islamic jihadists, for example, have proclaimed war against "the West," and they themselves are stateless rogues. This is why the threat of terrorism is so potent: there are seemingly no rules to it, and its violence can happen anywhere and anytime to victims who do not seem to deserve it. This is also why it is strange to declare war against terrorism, as if terrorism were an enemy state. In the political and cultural imagination of some observers on both sides of the divide, the conflict between "the West" and "Islamic terrorism" has expanded into a global conflict between two radically different worldviews. It has become, for some, a new crusade.

According to recent polling (2005), however, most Americans, do not perceive the situation this way: only 29 per cent think that the struggle against terrorism represents a fight against Islam as a whole. After 9/11, some were tempted to blame all Muslims for the attacks, but another reaction was a drive to understand Islam: Qur'ans flew off the shelves, books on Islam sold like hotcakes, scholars of the tradition were in intense demand, and undergraduate classes on the topic swelled. The drive to learn more paid dividends, according to the 2005 poll: the more informed the respondents were, the less inclined they were to think in black and white terms. Instead, the most

> "We are facing a mood and a movement far transcending the level of issues and policies and the governments that pursue them. This is no less than a clash of civilizations—the perhaps irrational but surely historic reaction of an ancient rival [Islam] against our Judeo-Christian heritage, our secular present, and the worldwide expansion of both."[13]
>
> Bernard Lewis
>
> "We are at war with Islam ... It is not merely that we are at war with an otherwise peaceful religion that has been 'hijacked' by extremists. We are at war with precisely the vision of life that is prescribed to all Muslims in the Koran, and further elaborated in the literature of the hadith, which recounts the sayings and actions of the Prophet."[14]
>
> Sam Harris

informed respondents (70 per cent of them) identified terrorists as a small, radical group—not as representatives of the tradition as a whole.

This result reaffirms the urgency of studying religion now. We should be clear that Islamic terrorism is hardly the only form of violence perpetrated in the name of religion; no tradition has a monopoly on it. So we can only hope to understand and perhaps even *do something* about these forms of violence if we inform ourselves broadly—and not just about those that grab the most headlines. To diagnose the nature of contemporary religious conflict, we have to know what's at stake for the combatants on all sides, and, in addition, we have to understand what religious factors have contributed *historically* to the strife if we wish to address our present concerns.

While violence and conflict are the most spectacular manifestations of religion in our current historical moment, it has also gained global significance in more subtle, persistent ways. Our world is becoming increasingly networked, mediated, and mobile: an average American, for example, is much more likely to come into meaningful contact with those who live outside of the United States (even if electronically) than ever before—and not just with other members of the "First World." The globe continues to open up thanks to technological advances in the transmission of information and resources, and as we venture further afield, we find that religion is often central to the cultural sensibilities of those we encounter: according to most estimates, at least 85 per cent of the world's population is affiliated with some religious tradition. As students, in our chosen professions, as global citizens, it is becoming more pressing all the time that we have cultural literacy with a worldwide scope—and studying religion goes a long way towards providing it.

The nation

Religion is also on the national stage *inside* the United States. You may be familiar with the part of First Amendment of the U.S. Constitution that says: "Congress shall make no law respecting an establishment of religion, or prohibiting the free exercise thereof." This proclamation expresses deep commitments that many Americans hold dear. For one thing, the Establishment Clause prevents government from supporting or affirming any particular religious tradition, thereby constructing an almost unassailable barrier against the establishment of a religious state. But the First Amendment also prevents government from interfering with the "free exercise" of religion and therefore contributes to religion thriving on the ground. Polling consistently shows that above 90 per cent of Americans believe in God, and for nearly two-thirds of them, religion is a significant priority.[15]

Part of religion's persistence and pervasiveness in the United States has to do with the deep connection between the history of the American nation and Christianity. But the U.S. has always been an immigrant nation, and especially in recent years, the religions found in pluralistic, multi-cultural America are more diverse than they have ever been. In order for Americans to understand themselves in this historical moment, to contend with their religious heritage and the challenge of religious pluralism, it is evident that studying religion must be on the agenda.

"Just as free speech and a free press distinctively shape and define American politics, society, and culture, so too does freedom of religion. By naming religion and marking it off for special consideration, the Constitution embeds the notion of religion in American culture. Because of the First Amendment, religion is a native category for Americans, a basic, culturally significant classification that we routinely and intuitively use to make sense of the world and explain what is happening to us. That there is religion and that religion matters are axioms of American life."[16]

William Scott Green

This point is particularly vivid when we contemplate the role religion plays in democratic decision-making about some of the most profound ethical issues the nation faces. While the Establishment Clause expresses a deep and very American commitment to the individual's right to be free of religious coercion, each citizen is also free to influence public policy based on whatever rationale he or she finds most reliable: for many, that rationale is *religious*. In the United States, religion (particularly, but not exclusively various forms of Christianity) forges the values that many hold dear, the "strong evaluations . . . discriminations of right and wrong, better or worse, higher and lower, which are not rendered valid by our own desires, inclinations, or choices, but rather stand independent of these and offer standards by which they can be judged."[17] Thus, when it comes to the debate about issues like abortion, the death penalty, euthanasia, stem-cell research, and so many others, religion and its "strong evaluations" play a major role. When school systems argue about whether to teach evolution or "intelligent design" in high school, religion is obviously part of the debate. And political leaders openly proclaim that faith guides them in their decision-making—and that is an important factor for many citizens as they cast their votes. In all of these cases (and many more could be listed), debate rages on, requiring a basic orientation to religion, which ends up affecting everyone in the American cultural and political community.

The United States is also home to some unique religious "types" that challenge and perhaps even disturb us in this historical moment. The dual commitment to individual rights *and* the free exercise of religion enshrined in the First Amendment, for example, finds expression in a class of Americans whom scholars have called "seekers." "Seekers" have a distrust of organized religion, and yet they recognize that the meaning religion has traditionally provided is desirable and necessary: it's a common truism that they want to *believe*, but they don't necessarily want to *belong*. Hence they tend to call themselves "spiritual," as in "I'm spiritual, but not religious." This perspective leads many "seekers" to an unprecedented openness and experimentalism with religion, and, for some, a synthesis of many different beliefs and practices. Of course, as observers we must wonder what principle guides this picking and choosing, and whether it can only lead to a fickle, superficial acquaintance. But the seeker raises important issues about the adaptability of religion, the American "faith" in the individual, and the role of *syncretism* (the combination and reconciling of different beliefs and practices) as a factor in religious change. Some seekers would predict that we are headed towards a unifying synthesis of the religions, within which all faiths will merge in one overarching system of belief. For now, that seems to be little more than a dream, but it is an interesting prospect.

The phenomenon of the open, experimental "seeker" sometimes overlaps with those who join new religious movements, but when a "cult" requires absolute adherence to external religious authority, the two types part ways. Throughout its history, creativity and division have characterized American religion: denominations and churches constantly split, combine, and recombine; new sects spring up, and even new religious forms make their appearance, often driven by charismatic leaders who have reconfigured belief and practice according to their own inspirations. On one side of the ledger, the proliferation of new religious movements, which scholars sometimes categorize by "family" (e.g., Latter-Day Saint/Mormon, Communalist, Psychic/New Age, Magical/Pagan, Eastern, and Middle Eastern),[18] is a testament to American religious tolerance, innovation, and creativity. On the other side, these groups have sometimes conceived themselves as isolated and oppositional, and when their members withdrew into communal forms of living that are radically set apart from mainstream American society, they become what many would call "cults."

The "free exercise" principle in the Constitution of course allows these groups to exist, but when the tension between the insular world of these communities and mainstream society (or government authorities) becomes too great, there is a flashpoint, as was the case in Jonestown, where 900 members of the People's Temple died by suicide and murder in 1978, or in Waco, where over 70 members of the Branch Davidian group were killed in the midst of a government assault in 1993. Why do people join these groups? What power do their leaders have? When do they cross the line and become something a society cannot tolerate? What do they tell us about the nature of religion? The American experience will continue to witness these kinds of groups, and the questions can only persist.

"Mainstream popular imagination has tended to view such [cultic, sectarian, or marginal religious] movements through the lens of exteriority, and the primary models available to the imagination for interpreting, making sense of, and coming to terms with exteriority have been the asylum and the prison. Alternative religious movements, therefore, tend to register within this imagination of otherness as either 'crazy,' 'criminal,' or usually both."[19]

David Chidester

With all of these comments about the First Amendment it is worthwhile to recall the Supreme Court's judgment about its application to the academic study of religion. That position is best represented by Justice Tom Clark's comments from the 1963 case, Abington v. Schempp: "[I]t might well be said that one's education is not complete without a study of comparative religion or the history of religion and its relationship to the advancement of civilization ... Nothing we have said here indicates that such study of the Bible or of religion, when presented objectively as part of a secular program of education, may not be effected consistent with the First Amendment." Clark affirms the value of both comparison and history of religions in understanding the "advancement" and development of civilization as a whole, leading up to its present moment.

In these pages we have only scratched the surface of religion's significance on the global and American stage. And yet it is clear that if we recall the religious past and observe the religious worlds around us, we will be much better informed as we attempt to negotiate the current historical moment.

Dwelling in a world of meaning

We began this chapter by reflecting on an interesting counterpoint: maybe religion is on the way out, so perhaps it's time to sell off our intellectual stock in it and move on to something else. All signs dispute this objection, however, as religion continues to *mean* something very profound in our world. The investigation of religious phenomena is in fact a study in meaning, as you'll recall from the passage offered in the preface (p. ix): "What we study when we study religion is one mode of constructing worlds of meaning, worlds within which men find themselves and in which they choose to dwell." That so many of our fellow human beings continue to dwell in these worlds would perhaps surprise figures like Nietzsche and Freud if they caught a glimpse of our historical present, and yet they could not deny what they saw: religion remains a living, thriving phenomenon.

This chapter has also attempted to suggest that the study of religion, for you, the student, is *itself* a "world of meaning." That may be so because there is something *religious* at stake for you: that is, you are religious yourself, and you want to gain insight into your own commitment through in-depth study and comparative analysis. But the meaning persists even if this is not the case. On a number of different levels, the examination of religion is meaningful for all of us, regardless of our religious standpoint. By means of the methodological principles we explored above (*self-consciousness, comparison, defamiliarization,* and *empathy*), not only do other worldviews begin to come into focus, but they also begin to give a sense of religious studies as a dwelling place of its own that necessarily means something to you.

If that point was not clear already, then it should be brought home by reflecting on our historical present. 9/11, the dominant historical event of our age, was so shattering because it challenged the worlds of meaning in which we find ourselves and usually dwell. It was a time to search for repair, and many attempted to do so by returning to or reaffirming their religious identity. Another response, the response of the student, was to *understand*, to sort out how such a thing could have happened in the name of religion, and to become a better-informed global citizen by gaining literacy in the religious traditions that are significant for so many of our fellow human beings. We continue to learn, and in the next chapter you will gather up more tools for building up your dwelling place in the study of religion—a dwelling that can offer some intellectual shelter during a stormy time in history.

Notes

[1] Friedrich Nietzsche, *The Gay Science*, trans. Walter Kaufmann (New York: Vintage Books, 1974), 181.

[2] Emile Durkheim, *The Division of Labor in Society*, trans. W.D. Halls (New York: The Free Press, 1984), 120.

[3] Sigmund Freud, *The Future of an Illusion*, trans. James Strachey (New York and London: W.W. Norton & Company, 1961), 43.

[4] Daniel C. Dennett, *Breaking the Spell: Religion as a Natural Phenomenon* (New York: Viking, 2006), 17.

[5] Gerardus van der Leeuw, *Religion in Essence and Manifestation*, trans. J.E. Turner (Princeton: Princeton University Press, 1986), 646.

[6] Hans-Georg Gadamer, *Truth and Method*, rev. ed., trans. Joel Weinsheimer and Donald G. Marshall (New York: Continuum, 1994), 299.

[7] Max Müller, "The Comparative Study of Religions," excerpt reprinted in *Classical Approaches to the Study of Religion: Aims, Methods, and Theories of*

Research, ed. Jacques Waardenburg (New York and Berlin: Walter de Gruyter, 1999), 93.

[8] Jonathan Z. Smith, *"Adde Parvum Parvo Magnus Acervus Erit,"* in *Map Is Not Territory: Studies in the History of Religions* (Chicago and London: The University of Chicago Press, 1993), 240–41.

[9] Jonathan Z. Smith, Introduction to *Imagining Religion: From Babylon to Jonestown* (Chicago and London: University of Chicago Press, 1982), xiii.

[10] See Mt. 16.23, for example, where Jesus, after praising Peter and proclaiming him founder of his church, turns around and calls Peter "Satan." Earlier Jesus announces, "Do not think I have come to bring peace on earth; I have not come to bring peace, but a sword" (10.34).

[11] Robert Bellah, *Beyond Belief: Essays on Religion in a Post-Traditional World* (Berkeley: University of California Press, 1970), 179.

[12] See pewforum.org/docs/index.php?DocID=89.

[13] The following scheme is derived from Bruce Lincoln, "Conflict," in *Critical Terms for Religious Studies*, ed. Mark C. Taylor (Chicago and London: University of Chicago Press, 1998), 57–65.

[14] Bernard Lewis, "The Roots of Muslim Rage," *The Atlantic Monthly* 266 (September 1990): 60.

[15] Sam Harris, *The End of Faith: Religion, Terror, and the Future of Reason* (New York and London: W.W. Norton, 2005), 109–110.

[16] See pewresearch.org/obdeck/?ObDeckID=15.

[17] William Scott Green, "The Difference Religion Makes," *Journal of the American Academy of Religion* 62, no. 4 (Winter 1994): 1193.

[18] Charles Taylor, *Sources of the Self: The Making of Modern Identity* (Cambridge, MA: Harvard University Press, 1989), 4.

[19] This typology is drawn from J. Gordon Melton, "Modern Alternative Religions in the West," in *A Handbook of Living Religions*, ed. John R. Hinnells (London: Penguin Books, 1991), 460–66.

[20] David Chidester, *Salvation and Suicide: Jim Jones, the Peoples Temple, and Jonestown*, rev. ed. (Bloomington and Indianapolis: Indiana University Press, 2003), 25.

2 Theory in the study of religion: An introduction

The first chapter of this book began by taking account of the powerful and pervasive phenomenon called "religion." We then acknowledged that this phenomenon inevitably means something to each of us, particularly in our current historical moment. Along the way, we also made some basic methodological preparations.

Now, to keep the project in motion, we need *theories* that will make this subject more intelligible. In this chapter, we address basic questions first. What exactly is "theory"? Is it even *possible* for *ideas* to bring religion into focus? What in general should we want or expect our theories to do? Are they accessible to a beginner? Are we going to run into problems in trying to apply them to religion? And what might successful results look like?

It should be acknowledged from the outset that the word "theory" might send mixed messages. For some, it conjures up startling discoveries in the scientific realm, the products of "beautiful minds" like Newton or Einstein. Maybe only a genius can come up with or understand theory, or maybe it has little place in the investigation of something like religion, which is not "factual." Others might associate it with unproven opinions or hypotheses, as in the common retort, "Well, that's only a theory." Many people think that a theory, even a well-developed one, is not much better than random speculation.

So, in general, what does "theory" look like in the study of religion? This chapter will illustrate that theories are hardly reserved for geniuses, and while they may not establish facts like those discovered in the natural sciences, theoretical approaches in the study of religion can assist us in the task of *interpretation*, leading to a better *understanding*. While there are some persistent challenges in applying them, good theories, effective testing, and keen intuitions can lead to better insight into religious worlds of meaning.

A word about the word "religion"

The English term *religion* has its origins in the Latin word *religio*. The term appears often both in classical literature and in the early Christian writings (many of which were written in Latin). But scholars are somewhat conflicted about the original etymology of the term.

Most argue that the term comes from a Latin verb *religare*, which means "to re-tie" or "bind again." In this sense, the term originally refers to the binding power of a religious tradition, the ability of religion to bind a community together with common creeds and practices.

Others suggest that the term originally comes from the verb *relegere*, "to re-read" or "go through again" in speech or reflection. This etymology would suggest that the term denotes a continual reinterpretation of some foundational source, like scripture. But it also suggests repetition in actions, perhaps rituals, and constant deliberation.

Finally, a minority view argues that the term was originally allied with an older Greek word, *alegein*, "to heed," "have a care for," or "be careful about." (The negative of this term would be "to neglect.") So religion is about something powerful (and perhaps a little scary) that demands close attention and constant care.

The correct etymological answer has no authority in dictating the way we use a term now, but each of these proposals raises valuable questions about what exactly the word "religion" refers to, which contributes to our interpretive options.

Theory in action: An example

In its origins our word "theory" comes from the ancient Greeks, who associated their word *theoria* with a kind of deep seeing. In other words, *a theory is a way of seeing something better in order to understand it, or looking beyond surface appearances to see the way something really is.* This might sound a little mysterious, but think about how we "theorize" all the time. Often in the midst of everyday debate, for example, someone will interject, "I have a theory about this." The meaning is clear: the person is saying, "I think I have a better way of understanding what we're talking about. Let me explain." Perhaps we gain some insight, but it didn't take a genius to get us there. We just needed a way to *look* at the issue differently, to *see* it more clearly, to get (closer, anyway) to what's *really* going on. The result may not be a scientific *fact*, but we have a better interpretation than before, and now we can submit it to further discussion and scrutiny.

So theory in the study of religion should be distinguished from theory in the natural sciences. As Ivan Strenski has written, "Nowhere can the study of religion claim to own anything remotely approaching a Darwinian *theory* of evolution or a Newtonian *theory* of the physical universe."[1] And yet a good theory is much better than random speculation or a lucky guess. The academic study of religion does share an important assumption with scientific approaches: theories are always subject to testing, both against the data, and by fellow researchers in the field. Because of this kind of evaluation, intuitions become transformed into "interesting and fruitful theore*tical* ideas, approaches, 'takes,' or 'angles' with which to approach religion."[2] As you will find below, as we take up the task of interpretation, "theoretical ideas" lead to a better understanding in four main ways: through *definition*, *description*, *explanation*, and *prediction*.

In order to arrive at this key point, consider the following example . . . and also remind yourself that *theorizing* isn't necessarily some arcane intellectual operation: it's something *you do* all the time!

About a year ago a young man (let's call him Kurt) started getting into trouble at school. His behavior became worse and worse, leading to angry confrontations with his teachers and the principal. Most recently Kurt expanded his exploits to include vandalizing a police vehicle, and now he's in trouble with the law. Yet he has remained stubborn: when the judge tried to scare him by threatening a stay in juvenile detention, Kurt swore at her in open court.

As an old family friend you know something about the back story: Kurt's father has always been a tough disciplinarian, and you've never seen him show his son any real affection. In response to Kurt's recent behavior he has simply imposed more regulations and punishments. Now the plan is to send the young man away to military school. Meanwhile, his mother remains on the sidelines (as she has always done), seemingly frightened of the intensity of the struggle between father and son.

What's going on here? What's your *theory* about this situation?

Obviously you would need a lot more details to feel comfortable making a firm judgment, but just to get things started, what do you think about this "theoretical idea"?

"Look, here's the situation: Teenage boys always rebel for a while. So that's what Kurt is doing. Don't worry: he'll get over it."

That's a reasonable suggestion: often the data confirms this judgment. But is it adequate for this case? It seems too general because it does not go very far in *describing* the nature of the situation, nor does it have much precision in *predicting* the way things will go in the future, let alone in determining what could be *done* about the problem. A more sophisticated theory is necessary.

A better diagnosis might look something like this:

"Here's my theory. This is a classic psychological struggle. It's his parents. His father was never emotionally supportive; he disciplined his son severely and never showed he loved him. And his mom, she just sits the whole thing out, and all along he wanted her just once to intervene. Now the kid is lashing out at authority figures who stand in for his parents. That's who he's *really* angry at. If his dad would just connect with him instead of imposing harsher discipline, and if his mom would just get involved more, he would stop this destructive behavior."

Maybe this observer is just playing TV psychiatrist, but even so, it seems that we are now making some progress. Why? What makes one theory better than another?

Let's break this theoretical idea about Kurt's situation down to get a better handle on what a solid intellectual approach *does*:

1. The theory presented above *defines* the problem first and foremost as *psychological*. An important aspect of any theory is its ability to *define* its object and area of inquiry. In Kurt's case, our observer has said, "When certain kinds of phenomena are observed we are dealing with a psychological issue." If upon further examination it was found that the young man had some kind of brain injury, and that was causing his behavior, the problem would shift from *psychological* to *neurological*. That would require different forms of explanation and expertise. But if the psychological definition is correct, then a whole range of appropriate theories and remedies become available— and prospects are improved for understanding what the young man is going through.

2. *Definition*, *explanation*, and *description* weave together. In this example, *psychological* explanation is based on a targeted theory: often when people find their wishes frustrated by family members (especially parents) during their upbringing, they will displace their anger onto others. Armed with this theoretical idea, a more insightful description of the situation is the result. Do the explanatory theory and the description that follows

have merit? We would probably have to investigate further (by talking to the young man about his history and his feelings, for example) to find out. At the very least, we have a *plausible* and *specific* hypothesis to work with, which will lead to *better* questions than we would have posed without it.

3. A theory's ability to *predict* will sometimes be its best testing ground. The theory about the young man displacing his anger suggests that if the *real* sources of it stop frustrating him, then he will desist from the bad behavior. It would be of great interest to the psychological theorist to see if this prediction panned out.

Now how does this discussion relate to theories of religion?

For one thing, while we should not begin by assuming that religion is a maladjustment in need of treatment, it is a *problem* to the extent that it is not always easy to understand. Kurt's situation would be messy, confusing, and complex in real life—and so (often) is religion, at least from the outsider's perspective. Note how the theory above sheds light on something that is initially perplexing and does it with a high degree of straightforwardness and clarity. Good theoretical ideas in the study of religion should do the same thing: a worthy theory of religion does not *simplify*, but it should clarify and present an eloquent response to its mystery.

This response takes shape as an informed *interpretation* based on *established ways of defining, explaining, describing, and making some predictions.* Studying religion is a matter of *interpretation* because it is always a task taken up from a particular perspective, and it is always subject to dialogue and dispute. But *definition, explanation, description,* and *prediction* are operations that build on the methodological principles described in Chapter 1 and stabilize our interpretations, leading to a better *understanding.* To illustrate this point, we will next consider them individually.

Definition

As we have indicated above, an adequate theory first delimits the phenomenon we propose to investigate. In that sense, *definition*, or the act of drawing boundaries around the subject matter, provides a starting point. And yet, as it turns out, this is one of the biggest challenges in the study of religion. While the meaning of the term "religion" may seem at first to be transparent, especially in everyday usage, further scrutiny reveals just how difficult defining it can be. What is it, after all, that we are studying? What exactly does "religion" refer to? Any answer, as we will see, is fraught with problems. But, again, some are better than others!

With a little bit of reflection, many of the definitions of religion that at first seem most obvious quickly get called into question. Consider one of the most common: religion is belief in God or gods that are to be obeyed and worshiped. At first glance, this proposal, which is found in many dictionaries, seems serviceable. Yet if we push a bit, it starts to crumble. The best initial test for any definition is to look for obvious exceptions: *if our intuition or common sense tells us that something is an example of "religion," and yet it does not fit within our definition, then perhaps something is wrong.* For example, the seemingly obvious definition above ("religion is belief in God or gods that are to be obeyed and worshiped") quickly runs into a big obstacle: Buddhism. Our instincts tell us that Buddhism is a religion, and yet many Buddhists, while acknowledging the existence of gods, find that they distract from the true goal of their tradition. The gods are not *central* for these Buddhists, which, according to the definition proposed above, is a requirement. So does Buddhism not count? Should we not study big parts of the Buddhist world if we are curious about "religion"? Or is it the definition that needs to be adjusted, or maybe even abandoned?

While we are often not aware of it, definitions carry with them a whole series of choices about what is significant, what is worth studying, and what is not: in other words, they include value judgments. If some strands of the Buddhist tradition do not fit our definition of religion, for example, what should we do with them? Leave them out? When something gets cut out of a category the message is often that it is devalued, in this case, because belief in God/gods is not central. Flawed or limited definitions have the potential to introduce distortions when they express value judgments about what they are supposed to name.

It is important to note that even if a tradition falls within a given definition, value judgments can still be present. *Definition has the tendency to identify one aspect of a broader phenomenon as essential, while everything else is peripheral.* One prominent scholar of Hinduism (who also happens to come from a Hindu background) has written about being asked to identify the most significant element in her tradition. In one case she said, "Food," because in India food is a constant element in festivals, rituals, and ceremonies. One of her colleagues responded, "Oh ... anthropological stuff," and continued by announcing that he was studying "religion" because his area of focus was "the Vedas," the foundational scriptures in the Hindu tradition.[3] As you can see, this response assumes a certain *definition* of religion, one that makes the distinction between *ancient scriptures*, which represent *real* Hindu religion, and the elements of ritual, which are merely "anthropological stuff."

The difficulties that arise in attempting to define religion might simply speak to an even bigger problem: generalized concepts, no matter how well defined they are, will never match what they aim to grasp precisely. One great theorist of religion, William James, offered a colorful illustration of this problem: "Probably a crab would be filled with a sense of personal outrage if it could hear us class it without ado or apology as a crustacean, and thus dispose of it. 'I am no such thing,' it would say; 'I am MYSELF, MYSELF alone.'"[4] More recently, Wilfred Cantwell Smith renewed this challenge: "religion," he argued, developed into a "thing" in Western intellectual life, "an objective systematic entity"[5] that fails to match up lived experience and personal faith. Smith even recommended abandoning the term altogether. Another Smith, contemporary theorist Jonathan Z., has his own elegant metaphor for this striking challenge: "map is not territory." In other words, the diagram that gives us a conceptual or schematic view of the landscape we travel never captures or reflects what that territory is *really* like. Perhaps the world, and especially the world of religion, simply refuses to bend to our will to define.

In light of the criticisms we have been exploring, perhaps we simply need to keep definitions of religion in perspective, while recognizing that they are vital and necessary: we need them to locate a starting point and to circumscribe our subject matter. If I am very curious about something called "hats," for example, and I want to find out all I can about them, I need a reasonable starting point to circumscribe my inquiry: "They're the things that human beings put on their heads for comfort, safety, warmth, or adornment." If I do not have *some kind* of definition, at least a working one, I might as well give up from the start: I could end up doing a very long study of shoes, or an intensive examination of sombreros (if my definition was too narrow). I could be missing the forest for one of the trees, or I might be in the wrong wooded area altogether. I need a definitional starting point, even if it gets adjusted and refined based on what I find later.

And that's the key: thinking about definitions as *provisional* and *adjustable*. There is an intellectual drive in the attempt to define that should not always be suppressed: the fact that we use the term "religion" in everyday language and have *some* idea about what we are talking about *should* invite curiosity about what *it* is. But the answers that we propose—and that theorists in the field have proposed—are but "takes" or "angles" that we should employ to the extent that they assist us with the task of interpretation and produce better understandings. At the very least, experimenting with sophisticated ideas about religion's essence will lead you to happily defy simplistic dictionary definitions.

Description

Whereas *definition* emphasizes the general and the universal, *description* focuses on the uniqueness of particulars. As Walter Capps wrote, description marks "the shift from singles to plurals."[6] At first glance, description does not seem to be too complicated: to describe something, don't we just need to observe and record what comes our way? A pencil and notebook (or laptop, perhaps) will do; no fancy theories necessary. But maintaining the focus needed to perceive all of the details of any given religious particular (a ritual, for example) is challenging enough. And then description intersects with theory as we attempt to discern the *meaning* and *significance* of what we observe. *Real* description, even of a single gesture, object, or person, becomes a complex act of interpretation. Below we will investigate two powerful frameworks for describing religion: phenomenology and "thick description."

In the previous chapter, you were introduced to the *phenomenological* approach. As you will recall, this method recommends "bracketing" our own perspective in order to let the data appear to us without filters or prior assumptions. Imagine an example of how this process might work. Think of a reluctant student who receives an assignment that he is not at all thrilled about: for his religion course, he has to witness and describe people engaging in religious rituals in three different places of worship. If this student proceeds in an anti-phenomenological manner, he will process these experiences according to a variety of preconceived notions: "What does the professor want?" "This ceremony goes against what I believe. I find it offensive." "This whole thing doesn't look right or sound good to me. It's ugly. And boring." etc. The descriptions resulting from these kinds of judgments will likely be biased and uninspiring. The student gave himself no chance to do a phenomenology.

If preconceptions are bracketed, however, the rituals appear just as they are, as phenomena in the world that rush up to us and require careful attention. But the phenomenological attitude requires even more than bracketing one's value judgments: it also asks the observer to suspend his "everyday" way of looking at the world. Think about this: the religion student goes to the same coffee shop every day, but has he ever stopped to observe the place with great care (the other customers, the sounds, the movements, the patterns, the taste of the coffee, etc.)? Probably not, because the coffee shop is hemmed in by a fixed attitude in his mind: "This is the place where I get coffee (and get anxious because I'm late for class)." Because the student is in the grip of this habitual thinking, he or she has never done a proper *phenomenology* of the coffee shop.

The *purpose* of this kind of bracketing and attention is description of the particulars, the phenomena that appear. So now, after bracketing value judgments and practicing his phenomenological attitude on coffee shops, our hypothetical student is ready. One afternoon, he visits a Greek Orthodox church, for example, and absorbs everything, through all of the senses, without judgment, without even thinking too much about what he or she perceives. People come in make a contribution, light a candle, kiss the icons at the front of the church, and they are on their way. The student describes them: how they look, how they are dressed, what moods, attitudes, and intentions they seem to express in their actions. In the meantime, the student also records the details of the church itself, its colors and the ambience. In the end the student has a richly detailed description of this religious site and what goes on there. This description, theoretically guided by the tenets of phenomenology, will provide the basis for much thought and reflection.

Another influential point of reference for *description* in religious studies is Clifford Geertz, a prominent American anthropologist who championed an approach called "thick description." In a famous essay on this topic, Geertz begins by telling a story: two boys simultaneously wink at each other, but one is experiencing a nervous twitch, and the other is purposefully giving a secret signal. Now a third boy at the table winks, but he is trying to make fun of the first boy's wink, which was (truth be told) a little awkward. How would we begin to describe and make sense of what has just happened? At the level of "thin description," all three boys have done the same thing by "rapidly contracting ... right eyelids." But at the level of "thick description," we would have to give an adequate account of what all these gestures *really* mean—and that would actually take some doing.[7]

Now think about what it would take to present a "thick description" of a religious event, which in all likelihood would be much *more* complex than the winking scenario. We would have to maintain attention to detail, and having experience with the religious tradition (and with similar rituals) would enhance the description dramatically. At the same time, a theoretical vocabulary would add perspective and richness. As Geertz has suggested, "any effort at thick description" starts "from a general bewilderment as to what the devil is going on," but "one does not start (or ought not to) intellectually empty-handed."[8] He later continues:

A repertoire of very general, made-in-the-academy concepts and systems of concepts—"integration," "rationalization," "symbol," "ideology," "ethos," "revolution," "identity," "metaphor," "structure," "ritual," "world view," "actor," "function," "sacred," and, of course, "culture" itself—is woven into the body of thick-description ethnography in the hope of rendering mere occurrences scientifically eloquent.[9]

The "made-in-the-academy concepts" that Geertz refers to here are similar to (and often the same as) the "theoretical ideas" that scholars of religion put to use in attempting to interpret their subject matter. In this passage, Geertz outlines the way in which description relates to those ideas: preparing for description requires gaining theoretical literacy, and then processing the data is intertwined with a vocabulary that renders our account of it more "scientifically eloquent."

In both cases (phenomenology and "thick description"), theory is interwoven into our ability to absorb and report on the particulars. To this extent, there is nothing simple about it: there is no such thing as "mere description" when it comes to giving our ideas about religion some content.

Explanation

One of the greatest television shows of all time was *The X-Files*. As its episodes unfolded over nine years, a grand mystery was laid out: first it was about whether extraterrestrials were real and had in fact visited our planet; then, once the first mystery had been settled (they *were* real and lurked everywhere), it was up to the main characters (and the audience) to figure out what the aliens were doing here. Every week, *everything* on the show demanded *explanation*: it was all about the intensely human desire to know why things are the way they are.

Religion is *something* like the UFO phenomenon: it presents the mind with a challenge, and many theories have tried to explain it. When it comes to encounters with mysterious lights in the sky, some theorize that they are in fact spaceships piloted by extraterrestrials. Others account for them in more down-to-earth ways, suggesting that they are optical illusions or natural phenomena, like ball lightning. On the one side the true believers—like Fox Mulder from the *X-Files*, who had a poster in his office that proclaimed "I WANT TO BELIEVE"—explain UFOs by asserting that there is *really* something out there, which explains the phenomenon but remains elusive at the level of concrete evidence. On the other hand, more cautious or skeptical observers suggest that natural or psychological explanations are simpler and more rational. On the television show, Mulder's partner, Scully, who was a medical doctor and scientist, constantly brought this rational perspective to bear.

On the *X-Files*, it was eventually revealed that the believer was right: UFOs really were alien spaceships. Such a concrete resolution is not to be expected in the academic study of religion. While belief in something that is "really out there" may provide adequate explanation for some, the study of religion has to test its results in the proving ground of the university, so "wanting to believe" is not nearly enough. Trying to explain religion in terms of one version of itself ("Of course alien flying saucers are ships piloted by extraterrestrials: they're alien flying saucers, after all!" "Of course religion comes from God. It is *religion*, after all!") will generally fail in the broader marketplace of ideas.

Over the past two centuries, the developing social sciences (psychology, sociology, and anthropology in particular) have contributed significantly to the drive to *explain* religion. From the social scientific perspective, explanatory theories "purport not merely to describe all religions but also to account for them" by identifying "the origin and the function of all religions."[10] In order "to account for" religion, theorists have often been drawn to *genetic* explanations that point to where religion first came from historically, or where it comes from whenever it appears. If we can determine why religion arose, then we will be able to understand what it is, in its innermost essence. At the same time, retracing the tracks of religion to its origin will tell us about both why it arose *and* why it persists: the social sciences have also offered an array of *functional* theories of religion, explaining it in terms of what purpose it serves for human beings.

As you can probably imagine, tracing the origin and function of religion is a very complicated matter, and the drive for explanation often runs into a much discussed problem: *reductionism*. While all theories attempt to explain one thing in terms of another, a reductive theory *over*-simplifies: it merely "explains away" an intellectual challenge too quickly. In the study of religion, Gavin Flood has identified two strands of reductionism: 1) within "cultural reductionism," religion is thought to be a delusion "that has served the interests of the rich and the powerful" and 2) within "naturalist or eliminative reductionism," investigating the brain tells us how "cognition and language" work, and "once we know how cognition and language work generally, we can know how *religious* cognition and language work in particular."[11] It is safe to say that explanatory theories about religion have often been closely allied with *skepticism* about it and a desire to see its demise.

And yet explanation does not have to be equated with reductive "explaining away." No one explanation can determine the universal origin and nature of religion, but taking explanatory theories as *tools* may be helpful indeed in interpreting particular examples that you encounter. Sometimes religion is deeply intertwined with economics, for instance, and needs to be interpreted in those terms. Other times it is intensely political; it is used to prop up a certain regime or ruling class. In other cases it seems to get its energy from a certain kind of madness: religion must be explained in psychological terms. And while it may be dissatisfying to explain religion in purely natural, biological terms, there is little doubt that it is tied to physiology. When it comes to explanatory theories, we must judge on a case-by-case basis and then reach for the right instrument, recognizing that as sensitive as it may be, no tool can fix *everything* at once.

Prediction

The final function of theory that deserves our attention is *prediction*. Being able to predict the future may sound like a mysterious operation, the province of fortune tellers and "media experts," but it is actually yet another way that theory is part of your everyday experience. Think about how much of your life depends on both tacit and consciously formed predictions. Based on our experience and knowledge of the natural world, we assume that the sun will come up tomorrow, gauge whether it is safe to cross a street, and possess some idea about how the weather will behave. Natural scientists have refined these kinds of everyday predictions, based on tried and true theory and method, and they can be quite precise in their prognostications about how the material world will behave.

Of course, human behavior on both grand and local scales is more difficult to predict. For this reason, perhaps, prediction is often de-emphasized in favor of description, explanation, and, more generally, interpretation in the study of religion. In comparing the interpreter of culture to a doctor, for example, Clifford Geertz suggested that both focus on "the unapparent import of things" in order to make a *diagnosis*, not a prediction.[12] But at the same time, for a doctor, delivering a *prognosis* is equally important, and in the case of the study of religion, our understanding is always directed towards taking a better, more-informed stance into the future. On a fundamental level, the study of religion attunes us to stable structures in religious traditions, such that *we are well aware of what will likely happen in any given context, and we know (with a reasonable degree of certainty) what it will mean to practitioners*, even in circumstances that seem strange and volatile to the untrained eye.

Consider the following example: imagine a "cult" group

comprising about 200 members, including about 50 children, has holed itself up in a compound somewhere in the western United States. Their leader is a charismatic young man who preaches the Bible for hours on end while his flock sits in rapt attention. Say that the local municipality wants to send in a health inspector, to make sure that the kitchen and sanitary facilities at the ranch are in order. Because of his mistrust of outsiders, the leader refuses to let the inspector in. The police arrive, and a stand-off begins, especially once the authorities realize that the group is heavily armed. After a few tense days, agents of the federal government appear, and they cut off the electricity and water supply, hoping to force the group out. Then they start bombarding the complex with light and noise during the night-time hours in an attempt to keep the members inside from sleeping. Finally, after 18 days, out of concern for the welfare of the children, the federal agents storm the building. When they make their way to the central common room of the complex, they find all 200 members of the group dead or dying from poison, which they took— or were forced to take—as soon as the attack began.

Obviously the federal agents failed to predict this outcome. They did not want everyone to die (especially the innocent children), but they proceeded on the theory that the leader was a madman who had in effect taken "hostages." Because they were simply "brainwashed" by an unstable personality, law enforcement predicted that if the group was put under some stress, members would begin to defect in large numbers, leaving only the leader and his most loyal henchmen vulnerable to seizure by law enforcement. But this theory was tragically wrong.

Later it comes out that a religion scholar from the local university had been observing the stand-off for its whole duration, and in its early stages he started to do research on the theology of the group and its leader. One day he decided to visit the site himself, and as soon as he saw that the group was in fact under siege, he had to speak out to the agents leading the investigation. After days of phone calls, he finally was able to meet with the agent in charge.

First he reminded the agent that *religious patterns* were at work in this situation: it was not simply a hostage stand-off, and therefore it would require theory that went beyond *psychology*. He argued that the religious orientation of the people inside meant that they were absolutely fixated on the *sacred*, something not of this world, something radically distinct from the *profane*, the secular, the everyday. The members' adherence to this principle, he proposed, came from a deep need for connection and belonging in a world from which they, as individuals, had become alienated. They had sated this hunger by belonging to the group, but it simultaneously intensified their distance from the outside world. In fact, they had learned to become afraid of its corruption and impurity. Because it had been purified by the group's leader, who was considered to be a man of God, the inside of the compound was "clean," while the outside world was corrupt and dirty.

Then the religion scholar described the theology and practices of the group in detail for the agent. To put it briefly, he brought to bear all his experience and theoretical ideas pertaining to *apocalyptic* groups, or those who tend to see the end of the world—or their departure from it—as imminent. The leader's long speeches pointed to the book of Revelation and linked his own plight and the trials of his group to the end-time described there. He began to interpret the siege by the federal government in these terms, and each new form of pressure was fitted to his biblical interpretation. Apocalyptic groups, the scholar suggested, often have an intense distrust of the outside world, and especially secular authorities. They also tend to maintain a dualistic philosophy, where the body and the soul are radically distinct. They propose that when the end comes, or when their end comes, they will be rescued and brought to a better place, and their death would be a message from God to the world and a tribute to his glory. In other words, groups like this readily become martyrs. *The scholar concluded (based on definition, explanation, and description) that if the agents continued to apply pressure that fit into the group's apocalyptic story, many of its members would commit suicide to achieve their religious goal—and they would force the children to do the same.* As the religion scholar revealed later, the agent remained locked into his own misplaced theory about the group's members being standard, run-of-the-mill hostages, and days later the stand-off ended in disaster.

This "hypothetical" scenario is of course a composite of the Jonestown episode in 1978, during which over 900 members of the People's Temple committed mass suicide or were murdered, and the occurrences at Waco in 1993, where 74 members of the Branch Davidians died in a fire after the ATF and FBI raided their compound. In the case of Waco, religion scholars actually *did* in fact attempt to make their predictions known, but to no avail.[13] The example suggests that accumulated experience, good data, and theoretical insight combine to make reasonable predictions *possible*, even if the powers that be are not willing to listen.

As a beginning student, you probably will not be advising the federal government during tense stand-offs. Also, in case you have received the wrong impression: studying religion has *plenty* of surprises, making predictions about it very difficult, as experts will readily admit. And yet you should still think about your knowledge as serving the future: as a family member, friend, neighbor, student, or co-worker, there's no telling when your familiarity with the theory and content of religion may come in handy, not only as a matter of *literacy*, but also as it relates to making predictions about the way things will go. And as a citizen, you have a voice about the future as it unfolds: keep in mind that informed judgments can be intensely *meaningful* in our contemporary historical moment, a moment in which religion plays such a significant role.

Insider/outsider: Orders of meaning in the study of religion

Everyone knows what it's like to be on the outside. Think about showing up at a party where you don't really know anyone—but everyone there seems to know *each other*. Or maybe you start a new job, or enroll in a new school. Even if you are welcomed in, everyone has their fixed patterns and relationships; they have their own way of talking and acting; they know things you don't. Sometimes it takes quite a while to understand what's going on, and then it takes even longer to become an insider.

The academic observer of human culture initially faces a similar problem. Studying a foreign culture in school, for example, is one thing, but actually encountering it in reality is quite another. Even if we know the language, another land does not give up its secrets easily, and most of us have to work patiently to see it from the inside. Some people take up membership in the foreign culture: they integrate, assimilate, and "go native." The academic observer also works to get inside unfamiliar cultures (and subcultures), but then adds a unique twist: as an outsider she wants "in" for the purpose of understanding but also hopes to remain distant enough to be neutral. This paradox, in which the scholar has a drive to capture the inside of other worldviews but must also remain aloof from them, is called the *insider/outsider problem*.

As you can imagine, religion intensifies this problem because *belonging*, being an insider, is often such an emphasis. As we have been describing it, the sophisticated study of religion involves stepping back; offering definition, descriptions, explanations, and/or predictions; and presenting an overall interpretation of religious phenomena. Obviously there is a difference between doing those things and *living* a religion. So if the representations of the academic study of religion are always going to be *etic* (i.e., outsider descriptions, like phon*etic* descriptions of how to pronounce words), how can we be sure that our understanding is accurate and true to the *emic* (i.e., insider experience, like phon*emes*, linguistic units as they are *actually* pronounced)?[14] Would someone have to *experience* being part of a religious tradition to understand it? Or is distance *especially* important in something like religion, where experiencing its interior would mean ... becoming *religious*!

Responding to this dilemma in the study of religion can flow in one of two directions. First: maybe our only way of interpreting the insider is *to be* one, or at least know what it is like to be one; having some kind of religious identity or experience oneself is necessary for one to understand. Short of that, perhaps the researcher's job is to let the insiders do the interpreting (because they are the only ones who really know what they are talking about) and to report on it faithfully. If the student of religion does generate an "outside" interpretation, drawing upon theories and methods from the world of academic inquiry, then the insiders have the final veto power: if those "interpreted" cannot assent, then the outsider's view must be discounted.

On the other side of the ledger, perhaps giving the insiders this kind of power defers to them *way* too much. After all, scholars often know much more about the history and variety of traditions they study than people who belong to them. Scholars also have distance and perspective; they can compare and analyze using sophisticated intellectual tools. In fact, getting *too* close to the insiders would be disastrous for the serious researcher: he would lose any kind of scholarly objectivity. At the same time, insiders only have their insular perspective. Remember: "he who knows one knows none." If that principle is true, then insiders have relatively *little* authority to talk about their own tradition, let alone religion in general—unless they are willing and able to break out of their worldview.

Some scholars have gone even further in emphasizing the scholar's control. As you will recall from the discussion of *definition*, it may be that the concept "religion" fails to map onto anything "out there" precisely. Jonathan Z. Smith has come up with a slogan for this difficulty: "*there is no data for religion*." Smith writes, "Religion is solely the creation of the scholar's study. It is created for the scholar's analytic purposes by his imaginative acts of comparison and generalization. Religion has no independent existence apart from the academy."[15] While this judgment may seem a bit shocking, we recognize that it is simply a splashy way of restating the "insider/outsider" problem: investigating something called "religion" is always at a distance from its subject matter, because what's "out there" never exactly matches the outsider's concept of it.

Four Orders of Meaning in the study of religion

The problem described here is profound, and whether you like it or not, as a student of religion, you are now in the middle of it. But *where* exactly? Differentiating "insiders" and "outsiders" further should give you a better idea. There are, in fact, not just "insiders" and "outsiders" in the study of religion: several *Orders of Meaning* are always at work.[16]

1. **The First Order, the *immediate*, is constituted by what "insiders" do, say, and feel, while they're in the thick of things religiously.** The First Order is made up of "[religious] expression which has often been deemed spontaneous, emotive, and uncritical ... [It] belongs to the realms of performance and ritual, and to the myth and symbol presumed operative within them."[17] It is also the layer of the text as it is read, recited, or expressed in rituals, ascetic practices, or contemplation.[18]

   Example: when someone says a prayer, like the Lord's Prayer in the Christian tradition, s/he is present in the moment and in the performance of the ritual; s/he is not busy with intellectual deliberations on the meaning of the prayer. In other words, s/he is in the First Order of Meaning, the *immediate*.

2. **The Second Order of Meaning, the *reflective*. Within religious traditions themselves, space is open for reflection on the significance of the immediate order that places it "within the broader scheme of what is deemed to be true."**[19] By means of theological, philosophical, commentarial, and legal modes of reflection, a tradition takes a step back from itself and attempts to organize its particular view of the world.

   Example: in the Christian tradition, theologians, clergy, and educators offer extensive examination of the Lord's Prayer and its meaning for the community: they participate in the Second Order of Meaning, the *reflective*.

3. **The Third Order of Meaning in the study of religion is finally that of the *academic*: it is the *theoretical* order that the outside observer occupies as he or she attempts to interpret and understand the other two layers.**

   Example: the function of the Lord's Prayer is to reinforce the social bonds between members of an immediate community (the local church) and the broader community of Christian worshipers (the Christian Church, with capital letters); thus the prayer primarily reinforces a sense of belonging for those who pronounce it. Such interpretations come from an outside, *academic* perspective, the Third Order of Meaning.

4. We should note that the *academic, theoretical* order of meaning can have something in common with the *reflective, insider* level: both have a tendency to posit a layer that stands *behind* the First Order because they claim to have discovered what's *really* going on. **Thus both participants and observers tend to create a *Zero Order*.**

    Examples: the Second Order Christian commentator may argue that the Zero Order for the Lord's Prayer is divinely inspired revelation and ultimately God himself. Meanwhile, the Third Order observer claims that what's *really* going on in the performance of the prayer is a desire for social bonding. All human beings have this need, so the *absolute* Zero Order is the human brain, which contains a feature, a product of evolution, that reinforces social behaviors.

5. **The Fourth Order of meaning is *your* order: the order of the *student*. It "cuts across all the other modes in reflecting the travails of one who must integrate them all in ways that are personally meaningful and communally relevant."**[20] As beginning students of religion, we are often participants in the Fourth Order of Meaning, so your job is to locate yourself, or parts of yourself, on different rungs of this ladder of meaning.

This framework gives rise to a number of challenging questions, but it also clarifies what people do when they discuss and wrestle with religion in an academic setting. Here's an example:

Let's say that after you finish reading this book you begin to study Hinduism, and you read some of the scriptures from this tradition, including a text called the *Bhagavadgita*, which tells the story of a warrior who refuses to fight in a battle against other family members. A god in disguise (Krishna) urges him to fight and eventually appears in his full, divine glory. In the end, the warrior is convinced and starts the massacre.

The words as they appear on the page are within the First Order of Meaning: they are *immediate*. A pious person may say them silently to himself; perhaps you go to a temple and see a group of people chanting them in unison. Still the First Order of Meaning. Now let's say that in class the professor lectures on the text. He explains the history behind it and provides philosophical context. Where are you now? Generally in the Third Order, right? But the professor is also *reporting* on a fair amount of Second Order *reflection* from inside the tradition to assist you in understanding the text the way *Hindus* understand it.

Now someone in class says, "I am a Hindu, and in my tradition these words are the authentic teaching of God. I will explain to you why they are authoritative . . ." That clearly seems to be in the Second Order of Meaning. But what if someone responds, "Well, that's all well and good, but this book is actually about keeping an oppressive society in place, keeping the poor people down. That's pretty much what religion in general is all about"? This person is clearly speaking within the Third Order, and he or she has definitely posited a Zero Order of Meaning that stands behind the book: it's *really* about economics and power.

Finally, here's the most interesting question: is it possible to be on several different layers of meaning at once, or to switch between them? Is that *desirable*, or is it better to pick one order and stick with it? Perhaps you, the student, will generally find yourself within the Fourth Order of Meaning. Think about the Hindu student trying, at first, to articulate the significance of the scripture on the *reflective* level. Maybe she now feels the impact of the Zero Order economic reality that her peer has tried to posit, and she articulates a response in the language of the Third Order of Meaning, in terms that are not familiar to her tradition. But then, when she goes to visit her extended family in Delhi the next summer, she repeats verses from the *Gita* with her grandmother and, for that moment at least, becomes a First Order practitioner of Hinduism once again.

So what is the right response to this complex issue? Who has the authority: insiders or outsiders? In the academic study of religion is it acceptable to move back and forth within Orders of Meaning (like the student above)? Can the person locked in the First Order study religion at all? That's unlikely, but can that experience be integrated into academic investigation? Can the Second Order commentator study religion with neutrality and objectivity? Again, unlikely, but does that Order of Meaning sometimes overlap with the Third? Can the Third Order scholar or student ever *really* understand? Maybe not, but aren't their broader perspective and intellectual tools *indispensable* for a world that is starved for balanced knowledge about religion?

Simple answers to these questions are not forthcoming, and yet the slogan "There is no data for the study of religion" offers an important clue about what direction you should take in thinking about them. In this statement, Smith reminds us that there are no *givens* in the study of religion, that we should take *nothing* for granted. When it comes to the "insiders," we should know whether their meaning is *immediate* or *reflective*. And if they participate in the Second, *reflective* Order, we should keep in mind that *they* have their own position in interpreting the inside. Then, pointing back to that crucial methodological point, we must be aware of *ourselves* when we study religion so we can be careful about bridging some precarious, but not impossible gaps.

Theology vs. religious studies

The study of religion puts some unique twists on the insider/outsider problem, but one version of it has caused the most controversy: what role should *theology* play in the academic study of religion? When placed side by side in contemporary theoretical discussions, *theology* and *religious studies* have taken on distinctive and sometimes contentious meanings.

In a narrow sense, *theology* is a Second Order practice that reflects on religion from within a specific community of faith and belief, particularly a Christian one. Christian theology has historically been at the center of the Western university, and today it continues to provide the foundation for undergraduate education at many American institutions of higher learning. In these settings, the curriculum might include courses on the Bible, the history of the Christian tradition, and the beliefs and practices of whatever denomination the particular college or university is affiliated with. Theologically oriented schools may also offer the opportunity to study other traditions, but obviously they will most often be interpreted in light of Christian concerns.

For those who want *religious studies* to be an academic discipline like all the others in the university (anthropology, psychology, English, sociology, etc.), outward theologizing (like insider reflections that espouse a specifically Christian or Jewish or Hindu or Buddhist or Muslim point of view) is not a valid way of approaching and representing the subject matter. At best, it counts as insider *data* for the *real* scholar of religion to examine. But in current debates, theology has come to represent more than the actual practice of arguing for a specific religious perspective: it is a question of the *theological legacy* that still lurks in many contemporary approaches to the study of religion—even those that *claim* to be neutral and even-handed.

The tricky thing about the academic study of religion is that it grew out of *both* theology (a Second Order, *insider* phenomenon) *and* the "scientific" disciplines of the modern university (the Third Order). Institutionally, theology was a driving *intellectual* force in the university for a long time, so its methods have often *overlapped* with those of "strictly academic" disciplines, especially when they have attempted to consider religion. In addition, the first religion departments in the United States (or their founders) emerged from divinity schools or departments of theology—this in just the last few decades!

So these observations have to give us pause. Perhaps the academic study of religion is still in the shadow of theology. Maybe Second Order insider approaches are still embedded within the study of religion. Is the study of religion just *crypto-theology*?

For some, these suspicions point to a legacy in the study of religion that needs to be purged. For example, it has often been argued that religion is a *sui generis* phenomenon: that is, it is a phenomenon that is unique unto itself, of its own kind and its own kind only. What makes religion unique? For many, the answer has been simple: "religion arises to provide contact with god."[21] That in itself is a theological claim: it presupposes a) that God exists and b) that all religious people pursue contact with the divine, even if sometimes they do it in strange or misguided ways.

Now, scholars of religion most often have not come right out and *said* that they believe that religion is about making contact with God; that would *expose* their view as theological, thus diminishing its academic authority. Instead, some would argue, they use other concepts to stand in for their theology and in so doing, have produced a number of highly influential "theoretical ideas" that continue to infuse the study of religion to this day: "ultimate reality," "ultimate concern," "the sacred," "the wholly other," "the transcendent," "the absolute," "thirst for being," and so on. Using ideas like these is basically interpreting religion in Second Order, reflective terms, some would argue, when what is necessary is understanding it from an academic distance, by drawing upon Third Order approaches such as philology, historical analysis, sociology, psychology, anthropology, and even the natural sciences.

You can probably see why the move to "purify" the study of religion of theology could lead to tensions. For one thing, the strong proponent of religious studies as a strictly a-religious project wants active theologians out of the picture. At the same time, the proponent of "reformed" religious studies also calls out scholars who *think* they are proceeding even-handedly but actually are not: because they are using "crypto-theological" concepts in interpreting religion, they are actually supporting or advocating religion itself. For some, the study of religion is *always* going to be tainted by its theological past. Perhaps it would be best to leave this subject matter to the members of other university disciplines: just having something called "religious studies" or "the study of religion" makes an affirmation that is tacitly theological.

On the other side of this theoretical divide, many scholars who interpret religion in terms of "theoretical ideas" like the ones presented above do not appreciate being called theologians in disguise. A term like "the sacred," for example, is broad and neutral; it does not stake any particular theological claim, but instead describes a human reality. Others take a more moderate view on the role theology might play in the contemporary academic study of religion. As long as theologians rise to the standards of the Third Order of Meaning (i.e., they engage in scholarly work, make rational arguments, and allow their views to be scrutinized), why shouldn't they be allowed a place at the table? Aren't all scholars and professors pushing a certain viewpoint? Why can't theologians do so in the study of religion, and in the broader university? As long as theologians are "team players" in the study of religion, then they certainly shouldn't be excluded.

At the same time, some theologians respond to religious studies by simply opting out, or, strangely enough, like their *opponents* on the opposite side of the spectrum, by recommending that the academic study of religion be abandoned. Theology is a *normative* discipline (that is, it aims for discernment of *the* truth and cultivation of *the* correct moral ends), and the mere description of religion hardly assists with that. Only theology can provide the answers. Indeed, if students want to *know* about religion they should return to their own tradition and *experience* its rituals, scriptures, and communities. The university should not provide them with a dim reflection of *being religious secondhand*: according to some, that is in fact what the academic study of religion is all about.

It would be impossible to work out all the details of this debate (let alone resolve it) in a chapter that is only designed to *introduce* you to theory in the study of religion. Yet it is vitally important that you are aware of this issue before proceeding. The past still speaks, and theology will continue to speak in the academic study of religion. And since the subject matter of the study of religion includes religious commitments, how could the commitments of the student of religion not be an issue? Some responses to these challenges are far too extreme: undermining the academic quest to understand religion in our day and age is unwise and borders on the irresponsible. A more moderate response will take the different Orders of Meaning seriously and, recalling the example of the Hindu student discussed above, will be willing to hear different voices—immediate, reflective, theological, academic, and theoretical—while also listening for occasional harmonies between them.

Conclusion

As a mere *introduction* to theory in the study of religion, this chapter has covered a considerable amount of ground. In asking and trying to answer basic questions about what theory *is* and what theory *does*, we discovered that it is far from mysterious, abstract, or foreign: it is an everyday activity that we are all familiar with. We also discerned that theory comes with a set of functions that have a great deal of potential when applied to religious subject matter: *definition*, *description*, *explanation*, and *prediction*. At the same time, we had to recognize important theoretical challenges that the academic study of religion faces: the insider/outsider problem and its corollary, theology vs. religious studies. Having thought through all of these foreground issues, you are now ready to consider some of the most prominent theories of religion that the Western intellectual tradition has produced in the next chapter.

Before moving on, however, recall the way we have talked about theory in the study of religion: you should always be on the lookout for good "angles" or "takes" on religion, "theoretical ideas" that will give you a better look, while constantly testing, picking and choosing, and adding your own insights. Note Clifford Geertz's position on theory, one that places *you* the student right at the heart of things: "Theoretical ideas are not created wholly anew in each study ... they are adopted from other, related studies, and, refined in the process, applied to new interpretive problems. If they cease being useful with respect to such problems, they tend to stop being used and are more or less abandoned. If they continue being useful, throwing up new understandings, they are further elaborated and go on being used."[22] In other words, when you examine, apply, adjust, and critique theories in the study of religion, you are part of the process Geertz describes: part of the evolution of the field itself.

Notes

[1] Ivan Strenski, *Thinking about Religion: An Historical Introduction of Theories of Religion* (Malden, MA: Blackwell Publishing, 2006), 342.

[2] *Ibid.*

[3] Vasudha Narayanan, "Diglossic Hinduism: Liberation and Lentils," *Journal of the American Academy of Religion* 68, no. 4 (December 2000): 762.

[4] William James, *The Varieties of Religious Experience: A Study in Human Nature* (New York: Penguin Books, 1987), 9.

[5] Wilfred Cantwell Smith, *The Meaning and End of Religion* (Minneapolis, MN: Fortress Press, 1971), 51.

[6] Walter H. Capps, *Religious Studies: The Making of a Discipline* (Minneapolis, MN: Fortress Press, 1995), 106.

[7] See Clifford Geertz, *The Interpretation of Cultures* (New York: Basic Books, 1973), 7–8.

[8] *Ibid.*, 27.

[9] *Ibid.*, 28.

[10] Robert Segal, "All Generalizations Are Bad: Postmodernism on Theories," *Journal of the American Academy of Religion* 74, no. 1 (March 2006): 157.

[11] Gavin Flood, "Reflections on Tradition and Inquiry in the Study of Religions," *Journal of the American Academy of Religion* 74, no. 1 (March 2006): 49.

[12] Geertz, *The Interpretation of Cultures*, 26.

[13] See James D. Tabor and Eugene V. Gallagher, *Why Waco? Cults and the Battle for Religious Freedom in America* (Berkeley: University of California Press, 1995). The hypothetical scenario sketched above also draws upon David Chidester, *Salvation and Suicide: Jim Jones, the Peoples Temple, and Jonestown*, rev. ed. (Bloomington and Indianapolis: Indiana University Press, 2003).

[14] See the extensive account of this distinction in Russell T. McCutcheon, *The Insider/Outsider Problem in the Study of Religion: A Reader* (London and New York: Cassell, 1999), 15–17.

[15] Jonathan Z. Smith, *Imagining Religion: From Babylon to Jamestown* (Chicago and London: University of Chicago Press, 1982), xi.

[16] The following framework is common in the social scientific literature; see Geertz, *The Interpretation of Cultures*, 15. My own version of it builds on Sheryl L. Burkhalter, "Four Modes of Discourse: Blurred Genres in the Study of Religion," in *Beyond the Classics? Essays in Religious Studies and Liberal Education*, ed. Sheryl Burkhalter and Frank Reynolds (Atlanta: Scholars Press, 1990), 150–51 and Flood, "Reflections on Tradition and Inquiry," 55–7.

[17] Burkhalter, "Four Modes of Discourse," 150.

[18] Flood, "Reflections on Tradition and Inquiry," 54.

[19] Burkhalter, "Four Modes of Discourse," 150–51.

[20] *Ibid.*, 151.

[21] Robert A. Segal, "Theories of Religion," in *The Routledge Companion to the Study of Religion*, ed. John R. Hinnells (London and New York: Routledge, 2005), 51.

[22] Geertz, *Interpretation of Cultures*, 27.

3 Classic theories in the study of religion: Part 1

We now arrive at an important turning point. Chapter 1 included starting points that pertain directly to your situation as a new interpreter of religion: *self-consciousness*, *comparison*, *defamiliarization*, and *empathy*. Chapter 2 outlined a further set of theoretically guided operations, *definition*, *description*, *explanation*, and *prediction*, that continue to bridge the gap of understanding between academic outsiders and religious insiders. The next step is to delve into the history of the study of religion to give these elements further shape and substance.

Why dig up theoretical ideas from the past, especially since all of the ones we will cover have been called into question? In academic disciplines, classic theories provide the basic interpretive vocabulary. Everyone in the field knows and has studied them, and even if a contemporary researcher rejects what has gone before, she attempts to stake out new territory by drawing out comparisons and contrasts with it. As the quote from Geertz at the end of the previous chapter suggested, the life of an academic discipline comes from the continual testing of compelling ideas, and if they don't continue to inspire and enlighten, then they will be abandoned. The theories we will explore over the next two chapters have not reached that point in the study of religion—not even close, in most cases.

The theoretical ideas in this chapter move along one particular axis in the academic investigation of religion: from the *individual* to the *social*. Eminent sociologist Peter Berger helps us add depth to this age-old polarity. Human beings, he argues, come into this world incomplete; we are not driven entirely by instincts, as is the case for animals, so *society* provides us with the rest of the structuring and order that we need. Thus society is generally "an area of meaning carved out of a vast mass of meaninglessness, a small clearing of lucidity in a formless, dark, always ominous jungle"[1] The individual stays in the light to the extent that his society is stable—and to the extent that he participates in its order and is ordered by it.

These observations first raise the most basic question: is the essence of religion located in individual consciousness or in the social order?

But then, assuming that Berger's characterization is correct, we also have to wonder: does religion reside in the orderly social clearing, or in more shadowy places, like the "jungle" of experiences, both within private individuals and lurking sub-groups, that broader society and its institutions just cannot absorb or understand? The theorists in this chapter present a range of fascinating responses to these questions, and you should take note of each one in all of its distinctiveness.

But before we proceed, a bit of intellectual context is necessary to explain how modern theorists were in a position to consider these questions—and the question of religion in general—in the first place.

The study of religion: A modern phenomenon?

People have been talking about what we call "religion" for a very long time, long before the modern period in the West, yet today we inherit a unique approach. For long stretches of human history (and this is still the case for many), it was difficult to find a stable place to stand *outside* of religion to get some perspective on it. But the cultural and intellectual situation in Europe changed that by the turn of the nineteenth century and opened up the possibility of a systematic, even-handed study.

A great number of factors contributed to this shift, too many to describe in detail. Here we can point to three developments that helped to get the modern study of religion off the ground: 1) the Enlightenment's reliance on reason and thinking for oneself, 2) the encounter with other cultures and religious traditions, and 3) the development of new academic disciplines, including the scholarly study of the Bible.

First, the *Enlightenment* in Europe had two sides to it: radical doubt and trust in human reason and experience. As far back as the seventeenth century, French thinker *René Descartes* (1596–1650) foreshadowed modern, Enlightenment values when he subjected all of his beliefs to doubt and analysis. In his *Meditations*, Descartes claimed that he would take nothing for granted and start with only what he could know for certain, which included leaving aside the data presented by the senses. The only certainty he discovered was famously *cogito ergo sum*, "I think therefore I am."

Eventually Descartes was able to reconstruct a world ruled over by God, and by means of analysis, he was able to break experience down, to understand its constituent parts, and then to put it back together again. But the grand gesture of subjecting everything to scrutiny resounded through the Western tradition. What *should* we "take on faith"? Should we in fact accept *anything* that we have not examined first? For the members of the British, French, and German Enlightenment movements, religion was the cardinal example of a human institution that needed testing: it had for the most part remained unquestioned.

Following Descartes, the German philosopher *Immanuel Kant* (1724–1804) was one of the great champions of thinking for oneself and resisting accepted traditions. Kant urged that we "dare to be wise" (*sapere audi*), and he meant that we must exercise our rationality in all cases, including when it came to religion. Religion could only be sanctioned when it remained within the limits of reason, and particularly when it promoted rational ethical laws, like "Do unto others as you would have done to you." As soon as religion strayed into what he deemed fanaticism or superstition, Kant balked. Reason is our only guide, and it can provide us with certainty in some cases, and in some cases (like "big" religious matters) it cannot. But leaping over rationality with religious feelings or intuitions was not an acceptable option.

As this impulse came to the fore in the Enlightenment, Europe also found itself awash in complex new data from cultures around the globe. Europeans had been encountering the rest of the world for centuries, but at the end of the eighteenth century a huge mass of texts, documents, and reports flowed in. Much of this information was the product of colonialism, the prolonged effort on the part of European nations to subdue and extract wealth from the far reaches of the globe.

The most dramatic body of information came from India, which England gradually colonized during the eighteenth century. The longer the English remained in India, the more of its languages they learned, and the more texts and reports they sent back to Europe. As this information piled up, it became clear that India was the home to a plethora of very ancient religious traditions, including Hinduism and Buddhism. Discovering the depth and breadth of non-Christian religion in India gave Europe pause: was it still possible to uphold the historical priority of biblical revelation as the original and only true source of religion? Was European civilization, which was thought to stem from an authoritative foundation in ancient Greece and Rome, the highest and most profound form of human culture? Or were there multiple strands of human civilization, each with its own dignity, and each driven by its own unique religious sensibility? Some European intellectuals embraced the discovery of other cultures and religious traditions because they seemed to represent a source of renewal; most derided them and thought of them as inferior, idolatrous, and primitive. Nevertheless, the mere presence of non-Christian religious traditions with complex histories, stirring rituals, and profound ideas all their own represented a significant challenge to European sensibilities.

Simultaneously, in combination with the ascendancy of reason and the in-depth encounter with other cultures, the modern European university flowered. The nineteenth century gave birth to many of the academic disciplines that we are familiar with today, including linguistics, economics, sociology, anthropology, and the study of world literatures. While the study of religion as an official academic discipline would not appear for over a century, the growing array of "human sciences" had a very distinct impact: more and more aspects of human experience and activity were put under the microscope, as objects that could be studied at a scholarly distance, through technical means.

That included the Bible. In many ways, a major taboo against subjecting religion to academic study was broken down when European scholars started applying historical, critical analysis to scripture. For example, the thought that the Bible was composed in layers, over time, by different people in different times was a rather shocking development for most denizens of nineteenth-century Europe. The profound ideas were still present in scripture, but they were linked to a time and a place, a *historical situation* that could be unearthed using ancient texts as evidence. Of course this suggested that the Bible was not the product of *divine revelation*—or at least not in the way the tradition had conceived it. This historical-critical approach also suggested that the Bible was one form of religious expression among many, one that could in fact be *compared* with the venerable texts that were flowing in from all over the world.

With this bit of history in mind, we are now ready to start inspecting the tools that the Western intellectual tradition has provided us with.

Religion as a unique experience

Rudolf Otto

As mentioned above, German Enlightenment thinkers often attempted to defend religion as a fundamentally rational phenomenon. They argued that a lot of it simply makes sense, especially from an ethical or social standpoint. For example, "Thou shalt not kill" is a reasonable moral principle that needs no supernatural source to recommend it: it is sensible not to kill without very good reason, because we would not like to be killed ourselves. Often religious rituals have reasonable aims also: if we are interested in building communities that live in harmony, for example, the remembrance of a great ethical role model (like Christ or the Buddha) promotes firm connections and mutual respect. According to some Enlightenment thinkers, these kinds of beliefs and practices were well worth preserving. But there were also aspects of religion that these same thinkers found distracting and irrational, and these, they claimed, should be left aside.

This highly rational approach incited reactions from Romantic movements across Europe. Romantics resisted the priority of reason and instead emphasized feeling, imagination, and nature. In Germany, this sensibility was most forcefully brought to bear on religion by *Friedrich Schleiermacher* (1768–1834).

Inspired by Romanticism, Schleiermacher identified *feeling* as the source and essence of religion. Religion, he thought, stems from an experience that links the individual with the infinite (God) in a feeling of unification. This feeling is expansive, overwhelming, and, as Schleiermacher himself described it, *oceanic*. In other words, when we stand on the beach and look out at the expanse of the infinite ocean, or perhaps when we gaze up at the stars in the night sky, a feeling of awe sometimes overcomes us. We are amazed and at the same time daunted. Schleiermacher proposed that these feelings are particularly vivid and powerful in religious settings, such that individuals who experience them feel absolutely dependent on something infinitely beyond themselves. Schleiermacher further suggested that this feeling may not be susceptible to explanation or expression, and yet religion cannot have any other source: there is no way that mere thinking can be its driving power.

Rudolf Otto (1869–1937), a German theologian and scholar of comparative religion, renewed many of Schleiermacher's views in his famous book *Das Heilige* (*The Holy*). But he also clarified Schleiermacher's approach and developed categories that prove useful in scrutinizing the experiential content of religion.

The Holy begins with a rather shocking recommendation:

> The reader is invited to direct his mind to a moment of deeply-felt religious experience, as little as possible qualified by other forms of consciousness. Whoever cannot do this, whoever knows no such moments in his experience, is requested to read no farther; for it is not easy to discuss questions of religious psychology with one who can recollect the emotions of his adolescence, the discomforts of indigestion, or, say, social feeling, but cannot recall any intrinsically religious feelings.[2]

Here we observe a vivid example of a theoretical dilemma described in the previous chapter: Otto seems to be saying that one must have *had* a religious experience in order to understand religion. But his point is also more precise. The center of gravity in analyzing religion, Otto argues, is not "ordinary" experiences like family conflicts, psycho-sexual development, physiological needs, or social bonding. For Otto, religious experience, or an encounter with "the holy," is *sui generis*—of its own unique kind, not reducible to other things.

"The holy," then, names the ineffable, irrational experience that is unique to religion: this experience is accompanied by "a clear over-plus of meaning" that goes beyond our attempt to conceptualize it.[3] Such an experience can only arise in response to something that is radically distinct from ordinary experience, an "unnamed Something" that Otto labels "the numinous,"[4] which first takes shape in con-sciousness as a feeling of absolute reliance on a creating power, as was the case for Schleiermacher. But the unique value of Otto's theory comes from his description of the "determinate states" of this feeling, which are captured in the Latin phrase *mysterium tremendum et fascinans* (that which is hidden, dreadful, and fascinating). The numinous at the heart of religion (the encounter with the "Wholly Other") inspires awe, fear, self-depreciation, dependence, and blank wonder, but at the same time it invites fascination and attachment.

In all of these modes, the experience itself is irrational; however, these experiences also generate rational correlates with religious concepts, which Otto calls "schemas." So, for example, the fearful nature of a god's holiness (the "overplus" in experience) takes shape as belief in that god's power, righteousness, and goodness; and the feeling of numinous fascination transforms into divine "love, mercy, pity, comfort."[5] Thus Otto provides a means of analyzing not only the irrational core of religious experience, but also the way it leads into doctrines, customs, and traditions: his own analysis treats examples from the Hebrew Bible, the New Testament, early Chris-tianity, Protestantism, "primitive" religions, Hinduism, and Buddhism.

You have perhaps surmised that Otto does a lot of naming of an experience that he believes is ultimately unnameable. This is because he had a rather unique purpose in mind for his scholarship, one that is in keeping with his strange injunction at the beginning of *The Holy*: he hoped to use approximate names and analogies "to suggest this unnamed Something to the reader . . . so that he may himself feel it."[6] In other words, Otto wanted his reader to *learn about* religion by *having* a religious experience, because otherwise it would be impos-sible to know religion at its core. For contemporary scholars, this motivation appears unabashedly *theological*. Inviting students and readers to become religious or to have religious experiences is not generally thought to be the job of the academic study of religion today. Nevertheless, Otto's contribution still looms large as a strong statement on behalf of the irrational, experiential essence of religious life.

Otto

The quote: "The feeling of [*mysterium tremendum*] may at times come sweeping like a gentle tide, pervading the mind with a tranquil mood of deepest worship ... It may burst in sudden eruption up from the depths of the soul with spasms and convulsions, or lead to the strangest excitements, to intoxicated frenzy, to transport, and to ecstasy. It has its wild and demonic forms and can sink to an almost grisly horror and shuddering. It has its crude, barbaric antecedents and early manifestations, and again it may be developed into something beautiful and pure and glorious. It may become the hushed, trembling, and speechless humility of the creature in the presence of—whom or what? In the presence of that which is a *mystery* inexpressible and above all creatures."[7]

What to look for:

- Irrational experiences that exceed the human ability to conceptualize them and also appear to be unique to religious contexts.
- States of absolute fear and fascination within rituals, in music or art, or surrounding certain buildings or spaces.
- The irrational, experiential core of rationalized religious doctrines (e.g., fear as the basis for religious laws).

William James

William James (1842–1910), the great American philosopher and psychologist, also emphasized the individual's experience in his landmark work *The Varieties of Religious Experience*.

One of James's fundamental assumptions is that individual, interior, non-rational experience is more profound than general, objective, or intellectual conceptions. He states, "so long as we deal with the cosmic and the general, we deal only with the symbols of reality, but *as soon as we deal with private and personal phenomena as such, we deal with realities in the completest sense of the term*."[8] So if we wish to understand the power of something like the Bible, then we must discern the experiences that generated it, "the inner experiences of great-souled persons wrestling with the crises of their fate."[9] In the same way, the founding of any religious institution, James proposes, relies upon an original inspiration, like a direct personal communion with the divine, "so personal religion should still seem the primordial thing."[10] And the same goes for religious belief. Belief in God, for example, does not come from intellectual proofs or systematic theologies; it comes from immediate experience. Like Otto, James tells us that the non-rational experience, one that is unique to religious contexts, is the energy driving the outward forms of religion.

Of course, orienting his study around human psychology opened up its boundaries considerably, perhaps even uncomfortably so. James was fascinated by altered or extreme states of consciousness, radical moments where it seems that the unseen, supernatural world wells up through the subconscious: "*if there be* higher spiritual agencies that can directly touch us, the psychological condition of their doing so *might be* our possession of a subconscious region which alone should yield access to them."[11] In his pursuit of these moments, James presents a remarkable survey of melancholics transformed by conversion, and "normal" religious people transformed into saints through their experience. In addition, he offers an extensive description of mystical experience, defining it according to four now famous criteria: 1) *ineffability*, 2) *noetic quality* (it bestows deep insight or knowledge), 3) *transiency*, and 4) *passivity*.[12]

But in all of this passionate analysis, one always has the sense that James was still a rational soul who hungered to have one of these profound experiences himself: he famously confesses inhaling nitrous oxide in pursuit of this direct knowledge. In the pages of *Varieties*, James comes off as a true American seeker who probably never quite found what he was looking for. But his categories continue to prove useful in our investigation of the kind of experiences he found so intriguing.

James

The quote: "Religion, therefore, as I now ask you arbitrarily to take it, shall mean for us *the feelings, acts, and experiences of individual men in their solitude, so far as they apprehend themselves to stand in relation to whatever they may consider the divine.*"[13]

What to look for:

- The individual, non-rational experience at the core of myths, scriptures, rituals, institutions, etc.
- The feeling of an objective but unseen presence, "something there."
- Extraordinary states of consciousness marked by ineffability, deep insight or knowledge (a "noetic quality"), transiency, and passivity, leading to a feeling of oneness and to a breakdown of distinctions, especially between "self" and "the world."
- The means of obtaining transformation: an interior feeling of bliss, freedom, and resolution (especially after considerable melancholy and suffering).

Religion and its social function

Emile Durkheim

Making our transition to thinkers who emphasized the *social* function of religion, we now turn to *Emile Durkheim* (1858–1917). Durkheim was a French social scientist and one of the most important pioneers of sociology as an academic discipline. He put forth his most influential "theoretical ideas" about religion in a 1912 book called *The Elementary Forms of Religious Life*.

In the opening pages of this remarkable work, Durkheim urges his readers to clear away their preformed judgments and criticizes some commonly held views, including the notion that religion is about belief in divine beings. Instead, as a starting point, he offers a pair of categories that have become ubiquitous in the study of religion: *the sacred and the profane*. This duality "is the distinctive trait of religious thought":[14] one realm, which can infuse *any* worldly object we might imagine, must be protected because it is somehow special and worthy; the other is associated with the everyday, the mundane, or even the unpleasant. The beliefs and rituals of any tradition, Durkheim suggests, essentially revolve around this duality.

Durkheim adds another fundamental idea, one that runs contrary to the views discussed above: "religion is something eminently social."[15] In other words, religion is not rooted in an individual experience because the social community generates all religion (and thus all religious experience) in the same way that an individual inherits a language he has not made: no one person invents a language; it is society that has done so. Similarly, all religious beliefs, rituals, and representations belong to a collective and only make their appearance in the individual. Without the collective, there would be no religious sensibility in the first place. In fact, Durkheim assumes that the very idea of the "individual," which has different forms in different places, is a product of social reality.

To flesh out these suppositions, Durkheim claims that it is necessary to go back to religion in "its most primitive and simple form."[16] A number of theorists had taken a similar approach, leading (they thought) to the moment when religious consciousness first appeared in the ancient, primordial past (see text box, below). But Durkheim proposes a different take: he does not aim to find "the very first beginning," the moment when religion dawned on humanity. Rather, its "origin" refers to "the ever-present causes upon which the most essential forms of religious thought and practice depend."[17] In other words, the origin is always present *wherever* and *whenever* religion persists, because it is a response to—it is caused by—a universal human need.

Three theories about the origin of religion

- *Primordial Monotheism*: Since the eighteenth century, when detailed information about the depth and profundity of non-European, non-Judeo-Christian cultures started to emerge, some made the argument that all religions had their source in a *primordial monotheistic revelation* that was global in scope: all religions were the product of an ancient, divinely inspired realization that there is one true God. Among different peoples, however, this belief eventually took on disparate, supposedly degenerate forms. In Durkheim's day, *Wilhelm Schmidt* (1868–1954) presented a "scientific" defense of this view, basing his argument on ethnographic information about the "Sky-God" worshiped by some Native American tribes.

- *Nature Worship*: Less theologically driven observers like *Max Müller* (1823–1900) started with the material world, and with nature in particular: all religion stemmed from fear of and dependence on natural forces, which led to practices designed to appease, manipulate, and master them. Soon individual features of nature (like the soil, animals, or storm clouds) were conceived to be divine entities, according to Müller, because of the way in which humans *named* them. In a sense, religion has its origins in a *"disease of language,"* where natural forces are named in anthropomorphic terms.

- **Animism**: Other theorists like *Edward Burnett Tylor* (1832–1917) suggested that religion began with the discernment of an invisible world, a world of spirits, souls, and eventually gods. He called this view *animism* and argued that it was the most primordial form of religion. Tylor thought that animism had its origins in two universal human experiences: 1) the sense that something invisible yet all-important leaves the body at the moment of death, and 2) the suspicion that dreams and visions make contact with a higher reality. Once the belief in a spiritual realm was established, it was only a few short steps to positing the existence of spiritual beings that stand behind nature, and behind the world as a whole.

Durkheim claims that the "ever-present" causes of religion are most easily observed in the so-called "primitive" cultures. Examining ethnographic data on the aboriginal tribes of Australia, Durkheim offers his own proposal for the most foundational form of religion: *totemism*. Totemistic religion is based on belonging to a clan, and further, on the identification of that clan with "a determined species of material things with which it believes that it has very particular relations,"[18] mostly plants and animals. So, for example, a clan might identify itself with the kangaroo, much as modern-day sports teams often take an animal as their mascot. The totem is a symbol of belonging, and so, among tribal peoples, it becomes sacred: the actual animal or plant is something to be protected, but it is really the *symbol* that is thought to protect the clan and bind it together. Myths and rituals surround the clan emblem, and its representation appears everywhere: on the objects possessed by members, on their clothing, and even inscribed on their bodies. Ultimately it takes on a life of its own: just as a nation's flag alone can compel its soldiers to fight, the symbol accrues its own influence.

As a sacred object honored by generation after generation, the totem possesses *power*, a concept that is central to Durkheim's analysis. Whether that power is named *mana, wakan, orenda, manitou, tabu*, and so on among tribal peoples, in each case primal religion refers to an impersonal force that stands behind the totem. Conceiving this power, which imbues all things that are sacred (including human beings), is "the source of all religiosity": even the gods, Durkheim suggests, are just "points upon which it alights."[19]

This is the moment where totemism and Durkheim's conception of religion as "eminently social" come together. The totem is, in essence, a symbol of social belonging. When totemists revere and worship their animal and organize their whole life around it, they are revering themselves as a community. As Durkheim writes, "if it [the totem] is at once the symbol of the god and of the society, is that not because the god and the society are only one?"[20] Often tribes construct ritual situations that are meant to instill this concept as an intense feeling of solidarity and belonging. These community rituals draw the individual out of himself and put him in touch with the sacred power of the totem, sometimes leading to trance-states, extreme behaviors, and "violent super-excitation."[21] Durkheim calls this experience *collective effervescence*, the experience of being swept away by the religious group.

For our purposes, Durkheim's most important move is to suggest that in essence, this analysis of totemism applies to *all* religion. *In every case, two functions are being fulfilled: first, religion provides a sense of social bonding and belonging and, second, it renders the religious community itself sacred and holy: it is made divine.*

Like many of his time, Durkheim took a patronizing view of his "primitive" subject matter, suggesting that it was characterized by its simplicity and naivete. His theory could also be criticized for over-emphasizing the social element of religion at the expense of the individual: this is where you as a student must measure his views against those discussed above. And yet Durkheim's analysis offers us fascinating tools for thinking about why, for example, many in a highly "individualist" society like the United States might be attracted back to religion: perhaps they wish to satisfy an undeniable need for community and belonging. Or maybe Durkheim's analysis diagnoses individualism itself: is it possible to make a totem of oneself? In addition, this theory also sheds some light on the root causes of religious conflict, intolerance, and fanaticism: group identification, driven by "collective effervescence," has tremendous *power* and can push individuals beyond themselves, to great heights and to unspeakable crimes—all in the name of their totems.

Durkheim

The quote: "*A religion is a unified system of beliefs and practices relative to sacred things, that is to say, things set apart and forbidden—beliefs and practices which unite into one single moral community called a Church, all those who adhere to them.*"[22]

What to look for:

- The significance of "primitive" religions; i.e., folk or indigenous traditions that do not fit into one of the major "religions of the world."
- The demarcation between the sacred and the profane, as expressed through rituals and beliefs. Practices that keep the sacred and profane separate or attempt to "manage" the power of the sacred: protecting against it and also inviting its aid or celebrating it.
- Rituals that cultivate a feeling of belonging; symbols or emblems that have a similar effect.
- The appearance of *power* in religious phenomenon, especially when it suggests the existence of an impersonal energy or force: religious objects that are treated as powerful by devotees.

Max Weber

Max Weber (1864–1920) was a German intellectual trained in law and economic history who eventually turned to broad investigations of social institutions. Along with Durkheim, Weber played a crucial role in the founding of modern sociology, and his scholarly attention often turned to religion.

Weber agreed with his countryman Karl Marx (discussed in the next chapter) that a basic starting point for understanding religion had to be social and economic reality, not grand theological notions. But Weber also agreed with Durkheim that religious ideas had a life of their own, independent from economic or political interests. Weber's famous attempt to bridge these two propositions went like this: "Not ideas, but material and ideal interests, directly govern men's conduct. Yet very frequently the 'world images' that have been created by 'ideas' have, like switchmen, determined the tracks along which action has been pushed by the dynamic of interest."[23] In other words, while the basic drive for power, status, and wealth may rule over human history, "ideas" or "worldviews" that come from religion can send it in a different direction from the one it would have taken.

One of Weber's most important works, *The Protestant Ethic and the Spirit of Capitalism* (published in 1904–1905), is devoted to this very theory: here we find a remarkable story about the influence of religious concepts on the way people think about work and money. In its earliest stages, the "spirit of capitalism" was defined by those who were interested in "the earning of more and more money, combined with the strict avoidance of all spontaneous enjoyment of life" [24]: Just think about Ebenezer Scrooge from Dickens' *Christmas Carol*, or Benjamin Franklin, who said, "A penny saved is a penny earned." In his book, Weber wonders where this ethos came from. He illustrates that the inhabitants of medieval and early modern Europe generally did not follow it: they did enough work to keep themselves in the position they were accustomed to. According to Weber, it was the religious ideas promoted by seventeenth- and eighteenth-century Protestants that made the difference.

The classic "Protestant work ethic," Weber argues, had its roots in a religious *calling*, a biblically sanctioned drive to work in the world in order to display God's blessing through wealth, while simultaneously denying immediate gratification in favor of more labor (which in turn produced more wealth). Marking oneself off this way was important for those who subscribed to the doctrine of *predestination*, for example, which meant that God had already determined who was bound for heaven and who was not: wealth was a sign of being chosen.

Thus a religious system with other-worldly goals (going to heaven) transmuted into the driving force behind worldly action. Such transformations occurred across the range of Protestant sects, and, as Weber demonstrates, some of the most influential early capitalists subscribed to these views, making them very successful. And everyone else had to buy into this new perspective, in fact, just to keep up. In the end, the thoughts of religious salvation detached from the spirit of capitalism, and those of us in Europe and America (and soon enough everyone else in the world) just kept working and earning, locking ourselves in what Weber called an "iron cage."[25] Capitalism had become an end in itself, detached from its religious origins.

In this famous (and controversial) analysis, Weber applied one his most important methods. *His characterization of religious contributions to the "spirit of capitalism" is an attempt to understand how the transformation could have happened given the world of interests and values in which early Protestants dwelled.* To put it Weber's terms, when applied to religion, his method of *Verstehen* (German for "understanding") required interpreting religion's "meaning" for those who adhered to it, with special attention to its "ideal types" or "carriers," the most representative adherent of a given worldview.

In keeping with this approach, Weber was fascinated by the individuals he called "religious virtuosos," the exemplary figures who devote themselves to their respective religious pathways. Such virtuosos might include public religious authorities like priests, rabbis, imams, or Brahmins, those who serve a community and interact with the larger world beyond. Hence one of Weber's categories, *priestly religion*. But some of the most interesting virtuosos are those who tend to take a more extraordinary approach to attaining their goals: *mystics* and *ascetics*. Mystics, Weber claimed, base their quest on inward experience and seek contemplative, non-rational union with the divine, leading them to flee from the world. Ascetics often follow the same path by retiring from the world in monasteries and ashrams, but they actively strive for self-mastery, often "subjecting the natural drives to a systematic patterning of life" in order to become an "instrument of god."[26] The *prophet* was another prominent type, the figure who "proclaims a religious doctrine or divine commandment" with authority, sometimes calling for a new religious sensibility, sometimes renewing the old.[27] Examples include Muhammad, the Buddha, and Jesus, who all drew upon their own inner talents to construct "a unified view of the world derived from consciously integrated and meaningful attitude toward life."[28]

It should be noted that Weber often used these categories to characterize a given religious tradition as a whole, or a religious tradition at a given stage. That is, some religions seem to be particularly "priestly" in character, some "ascetic," and so on. At the same time, a religion may have "prophetic" origins, but then it becomes dominated by some other strand. So Weber also employed these categories to account for the complexity of change and development, both as a product of outside influences, and as a phenomenon interior to religious communities.

One of the most interesting ways Weber talked about change is directly related to the nature of religious virtuosos: What is the power that stands behind the most influential of these exemplary types? Weber called it *charisma*, the "*extraordinary* quality of a person, regardless of whether this quality is actual, alleged, or presumed."[29] But charisma is fleeting because it is attached to an individual: a charismatic prophet, for example, preaches his great, sometimes radical message, gathers a following interested in change and reform, and then inevitably dies. What is the community to do in order for the message to persist through time, after the prophet's departure from the world?

Weber's answer: *routinization*. It is crucial to institutionalize the radical and spontaneous eruption of the prophet, to "bottle" the charisma so the movement of the prophet persists. You will notice that there is a tension between a spontaneous, radical, and charismatic individual and that which characterizes routinization: bureaucracy, routines, meetings, logistics, money, etc. However, various practices, including communal rituals, preaching, and pastoral care are meant to recapture the message and charisma of the prophet, even though that individual is long gone.

This has only been a very limited sampling of what Weber had to say, but you can see that he focused on the ways in which religion *means something* to its adherents. Ultimately religion is *all about meaning* for him: at the core of the Weberian analysis is the problem of suffering, the fact that terrible things happen to very good or even innocent people, and that bad people quite often get away scot-free. Weber argues that all religions provide a response to this issue, in the end laying out a "stand" against a world that often seems "senseless": the religious "demand" is "that the world order in its totality is, could, and should somehow be a meaningful 'cosmos'".[30]

Despite this final emphasis on meaning, it is not easy to nail down a clear, singular theory of religion in Weber's work. But we have discovered a rich array of "theoretical ideas" to work with here because Weber always made an exhaustive attempt to examine a worldview through and through, to see it as a living response to questions that all human beings face, and finally, to discern the way it makes sense given the interests of those who uphold it. It sometimes seems that Weber took some private joy in calling many religious forms "rational"—just because he knew that doing so would irritate the rational, scientific enemies of religion. Of course, Weber had his own sense of the term: something is "rational" when it makes practical or systematic sense within the parameters of a certain problem. When the big questions are on the table, he proposed, religion has often provided the most rational response.

Weber

The quote: "Religious postulates can come into conflict with the 'world' from differing points of view, and the point of view involved is always of the greatest importance for the direction and for the way in which *salvation* will be striven for. At all times and in all places, the need for salvation ... has resulted from the endeavor of a systematic and practical rationalization of life's realities ... [A]ll religions have demanded a specific presupposition that the course of the world be somehow *meaningful*, at least in so far as its touches upon the interests of men. As we have seen, this claim naturally emerged first as the customary problem of unjust suffering, and hence as the postulate for a just compensation for the unequal distribution of individual happiness in the world."[31]

What to look for:

- The interaction between religion and other human interests and realities, particularly economics and politics.
- Examples of Weber's *ideal types*, *carriers*, and *virtuosos*: priests, prophets, ascetics, and mystics.
- The interplay between *charisma* and *routinization*. Who has *charisma* and how is it recognized? How does a tradition recapture the *charisma* of its founder?
- How does a religion make sense or represent a "rational" response to both "everyday" economic and political circumstances, and to basic questions of meaning, especially the problem of unwarranted suffering in the world?

Victor Turner

In addition to sociologists like Durkheim and Weber, anthropologists have also made considerable contributions to our understanding of religion. A good example is Victor Turner (1920–83), who engaged in fieldwork in Africa and developed a highly influential theory of ritual.

Turner based his theory on the work of an earlier anthropologist, the Belgian *Arnold van Gennep* (1873–1957). Van Gennep focused on "rites of passage," rituals that "accompany a passage from one situation to another or from one cosmic or social world to another."[32] Such practices mark individual transitions, such as birth, coming of age, marriage, pregnancy, going on or coming home from a big journey, initiation, going into a holy area, or funerals. "Cosmic" rites of transition might also celebrate the change of seasons, the harvest, or the New Year, and "social" rituals go along with events like the transfer of political authority or the declaration of war. To scrutinize such practices, van Gennep introduced a useful set of categories: rites of passage all include a "preliminal" stage (associated with "separation"), a "liminal" stage (associated with "transition"), and a "post-liminal" stage (associated with "incorporation").[33]

What exactly do these categories describe? First it is necessary to define the term "liminal," which is central to van Gennep's theory. The adjective comes from the Latin word *limen*, which means "threshold," as in the doorway of a house. So, first, the *preliminal* stage of a rite of passage is often characterized by *separation from normal life*. Separation is often associated with purification and preparation for undergoing the ritual. In the middle realm, the *liminal* stage itself, rites marking the *transition* are central, and they can be quite attention-grabbing: some tribal coming of age rituals, for example, include wearing special clothing or cutting the hair; others have more permanent effects, including tattooing, scarifying, knocking out a tooth, or even cutting off the end of a finger. Acts like these radically mark the transition from one status to another (for example, child to young adult). Finally, the third, *postliminal* stage ushers the participant back into society and *incorporates* him or her once again, but now with a new status and identity. Social celebrations that symbolize unity and reunification often mark this stage.

As van Gennep made clear, this is only a general schema: in most rituals, one of these elements is more pronounced than the others, so any given example may emphasize separation, transition, or incorporation over the others. Nevertheless, "a typical pattern always recurs: *the pattern of the rites of passage*."[34]

Victor Turner built on van Gennep's theory but then added his own particular emphasis. To cite one of Turner's favorite examples, when someone goes on a *pilgrimage* symbolic gestures often mark the beginning of the holy journey, indicating *separation* from the normal and the everyday. And surely it is crucial to have rituals that help welcome the pilgrim home again, allowing him or her to *reincorporate* back into the community. But what exactly happens in the heart of the journey, at the pilgrimage site itself, a "place and moment 'in and out of time'"?[35] Why does the pilgrim expect to have an encounter with the sacred there, while in the *liminal* phase of the journey—the phase that seems to generate the power of so many rituals?

First and foremost, according to Turner, rituals often open up a space where participants are "neither here nor there": they are "betwixt and between" the usual status assigned to them in everyday society; [36] they are liberated from the constraints of the everyday because they are "outside or on the peripheries of everyday life."[37] So in a coming of age ritual, for example, those separated in preparation for the ceremony are neither children nor adults: they are not recognizable, and sometimes the community treats them that way. Being released from one's usual social self provides an occasion for reflection at a vital moment of transition, but ritual, according to Turner, is not primarily about the individual, for everyone in the liminal group is in the same boat: everyone is "betwixt and between." The participants are stripped of identity and status, remain submissive to the leaders of the ritual, and display great homogeneity amongst themselves (maybe they all wear the same costume or undergo the same ritual hardships). These circumstances lead to a tremendous feeling of "intense comradeship and egalitarianism"[38]—regardless of who or what the participants are in everyday life.

Turner calls this feeling *communitas*, which can be a vital product of liminality. We might call this "bonding," but Turner pushes the idea further. Everyday social existence is a realm of structures and hierarchies. It's a realm of who's who, determined by an array of distinguishing characteristics, like those you might put on a census form, and, on another level, by a social scale of wealth, prestige, and power. All of this is necessary for complex societies to hold themselves together, but it also has a downside: "Structure is all that holds people apart, defines their differences, and constrains their actions."[39] The liminal space in ritual, in contrast, opens up a realm of *anti-structure*, for "communitas emerges where social structure is not."[40] By stripping away everyday identities and mixing up social categories, participants are reminded of "an essential and generic bond" upon which society itself is founded: "the high could not be high unless the low existed, and he who is high must experience what it is like to be low."[41]

While the counter-cultural, anti-structural character of liminality can confront or even threaten the normal functioning of a religious or social orthodoxy, Turner directs our attention to just how often it is encouraged. Communitas sometimes springs up without much warning or planning, producing what Turner calls *existential* or *spontaneous* communitas. But quite often religious traditions sanction and carefully construct liminal occasions, producing *normative* communitas. Such occasions have distinct value. For one thing, they provide a relief from the everyday: Mardi Gras is an example of a liminal event that has a cathartic effect for thousands each year. In a religious context, this release has deeper significance: it reminds the religious person that adherence is a question of choice, that he or she could live otherwise, and thus remaining in the fold after the ritual renews one's commitment. In addition, as we have seen, it re-forges a sense of common social identity, a feeling of "humankindness" and solidarity that is most often missing in everyday life. It also opens a space for creativity, innovation, and change: because it is an indeterminate, anti-structural realm of experience, it is full of potential. Freed from everyday "clichés," social status, and "role playing," those in the *limen* have a chance to think things anew[42] and perhaps bring new insights back into the tradition or society to which they belong. One might go so far as to say that all great developments in human consciousness arise from a liminal space. Figures like Jesus and the Buddha were certainly "betwixt and between," and they called for communitas and anti-structure in the midst of rigid, hierarchical societies.

This state is so prized that a religion (and sometimes whole societies) will support the existence of permanent, liminal institutions. Turner cites the example of monks and nuns (say, in Christianity or Buddhism) who establish egalitarian communities and eschew the structures of everyday social life. Such groups have historically provided an escape from the constraints of social existence, while also reminding religions about their core values and identity. In modern society, Turner suggests, non-religious liminal groups have sometimes served a similar function. Counter-cultural artists, for example, who have at times chosen a life of relative poverty and communal living, have produced powerful insights. At the same time, in modern, largely secularized societies of the West, religions as a whole open up perennial, liminal spaces that serve as realms of anti-structure and communitas in a highly bureaucratic and compart-mentalized world.

Turner generated his theory of the ritual process in the late 1960s, and it shows: he often associated liminality and *communitas* with "hippies" and "beats," "who 'opt out' of the status-bound social order"[43] in order to have "a transformative experience that goes to the root of each person's being and finds in that root something profoundly communal and shared."[44] To this extent, Turner's theory is somewhat romantic, for as he suggested, rituals and counter-cultures have the tendency to reinforce our common humanity—and not our divisions. Nevertheless, in his account of the liminal stage of religious practice and ritual activity, Turner provides us with a theory that attempts to explain where *the sacred core* of religious life often comes from: from ritual, he proposes, and in particular, from rituals that mix up our everyday expectations and existence. Only in a liminal space, Turner claims, do higher realities truly speak.

Turner

The quote: "The great historical religions have, in the course of time, learned how to incorporate enclaves of communitas within their institutionalized structures—just as tribal religions do with their *rites de passage*—and to oxygenate, so to speak, the 'mystical body' by making provisions for those ardent souls who wish to live in communitas and poverty all their lives. Just as in a ritual of any complexity there are phases of separation from and reaggregation to the domain of the social structure ... and a liminal phase representing an interim of communitas ... so does a great religion or church contain many organizational and liturgical sectors which ... maintain in a central position a sanctuary of unqualified communitas ... "[45]

What to look for:

- Ritual in its many forms, especially "rites of passage": birth, coming of age, marriage, initiation, funerals, etc.
- The structure of specific rituals: separation, liminality, and reincorporation/reaggregation.
- The power of liminality: communitas and anti-structure at the heart of ritual.
- Perennial liminal institutions that have developed within a religion.
- Pilgrimage as a particularly vivid example of the theory.

Clifford Geertz

In the previous chapter you already explored an idea proposed by American anthropologist Clifford Geertz (1926–2006): "thick description." Geertz specified the theory behind applying this practice of religion in a well-known essay entitled "Religion as a Cultural System."

Geertz begins with some thoughts that we have already run across: religion is a part of culture, and as such, it is part of a "historical transmitted pattern of meanings embodied in symbols . . . by means of which men communicate, perpetuate, and develop their knowledge about and attitudes toward life."[46] But what is unique to religion as a significant manifestation of human culture? How specifically does it fit into the bigger puzzle of cultural meaning?

First, religion is "a system of symbols." Symbols are "tangible" and "perceptible" things that stand in for abstractions like "ideas, attitudes, judgments, longings, or beliefs."[47] Examples include everything from the written number "6" to the cross in Christianity. But Geertz also says that a religion is a "*system* of symbols," so it is a grouping of symbols that hang together in a set of relatively stable and reliable relationships, much like a language. So we should think of the Christian cross *and* all of the other symbols associated with the passion of Jesus Christ, for example, and the relation between *that* set of symbols and all the other sets within the Christian tradition, and so on. Because they include these kinds of complex networks of symbolic meaning, religious traditions provide a comprehensive map of the world and how to live in it.

Geertz captures this capacity of a "system" like religion by saying that it provides both "models of" and "models for." "Models of" describe or give a representation of the world, like a model of an atom or a map, and "models for" are like a blueprint for a building that has not yet been constructed: they tell us *how* to do it. As a "system of symbols," religion provides both a *model of* the world we inhabit (it describes it) and a *model for* our activity in the world (it recommends how to shape it).

Geertz also emphasizes the unique way a religious symbol system takes root: it produces "powerful, pervasive, and long-lasting moods and motivations."[48] A religion cultivates a mind-set that keeps its participants invested. Through practice, upbringing, and ritual, it cultivates "motivations," different directions in character like "moral circumspection" or "dispassionate tranquility," and "moods," temporary mental states that are attached to the symbols of the religious system.[49] In these ideas Geertz attempts to bring together the impersonal, inherited realm of religion as a symbolic system (no individual Christian "thinks up" a symbol like the cross: it is a given from the beginning) and the individual's experience of a tradition.

Why does a seemingly impersonal system of symbols, which after all are merely objects that stand in for abstractions, have the power to evoke powerful moods and motivations? Borrowing from Weber, Geertz claims that a coherent religious system provides a sense of order in a world that often threatens us with meaninglessness: this is in fact what ultimately differentiates religion from other cultural structures. A religion "must ... affirm something," "some transcendent truths" that can account for seeming anomalies and absurdities in life.[50] Again, like Weber, the most serious challenge that a religion confronts is the problem of seemingly unwarranted suffering, where bad things happen to good people and vice versa. But Geertz adds his own twist. The challenge of a religious system of meaning, he says, is not to resolve the problem or even to avoid suffering. Rather, as an ordered system of reliable ideas about the world that *also* evokes "moods and motivations," a religion helps its followers "make of physical pain, personal loss, worldly defeat, or the helpless contemplation of others' agony something bearable, supportable—something, as we say, sufferable."[51] In fact, in exploring the gap between the ways things *are* and the way they *ought* to be, religions may actually celebrate it—as long as there are powerful symbols that can come to the rescue and at least *account for* the elusive nature of the answers to our big questions.

Finally, Geertz wonders about why religious people come to believe in all of this stuff in the first place. If the sense of order that religion as a cultural system bestows is in constant danger, why buy into it? Where does religion's "aura of factuality" come from? Why does it seem *true* for so many? The authority of religion can come from many places, including long-standing traditions, individual experience, charismatic leaders, or revealed scriptures, but everything,

Geertz claims, depends on taking up the religious perspective, which can be boiled down to a simple formula: "he who would know must first believe."[52] The primary way belief is cultivated in religion is *ritual*: "For it is in ritual ... that this conviction that religious conceptions are veridical [true] and that religious directives are sound is somehow generated."[53] In ritual everything in the system meets up: the symbols, the "models of" the world and "models for" life, the "moods and motivations" are evoked, and a sense of order and meaning is cultivated.

You can probably see how "thick" a description of any given religious phenomena will have to be if it takes Geertz's theory as a starting point. Complex symbol systems and their relation to other symbol systems need our attention, as do the "moods and motivations" of individual practitioners. The Weberian challenge, the "problem of meaning," also calls out for examination, so we have to be on top of our philosophical game as well. And finally, if that's not enough, we have to learn how to read rituals in all their meaning and significance for communities and practitioners. Obviously Geertz's theory of religion is not for the shy; it puts the ball in our court and challenges us to delve into the "thickness" of religion. That is surely its greatest merit: there's no shortage of compelling "theoretical ideas" here that usher us into the subject matter, which (as Geertz reminds us) is intriguing precisely because it is so complex.

Geertz

The quote: "... a *religion* is: (1) a system of symbols which acts to (2) establish powerful, pervasive, and long-lasting moods and motivations in men by (3) formulating conception of a general order of existence and (4) clothing these conceptions with such an aura of factuality that (5) the moods and motivations seem uniquely realistic."[54]

What to look for: *Thick Description*

- Religious symbols that form a coordinated, interlocking system of meaning for adherents.
- The moods and motivations a religion promotes, and how it cultivates them.
- A religion's response to the "Problem of Meaning". How does it teach the believer "how to suffer"? Does it identity the line between the way the world *is* as opposed to what it *ought* to be? How does it contend with that dilemma?
- The means of generating an "aura of factuality" in a religion, especially by means of ritual.

Conclusion: Welcome to the jungle

So where does religion essentially reside, in the experience of the individual, or in the structures of society? And further, does it open up a bright, ordered clearing, or does it come from out there, in the shadowy jungle of the non-rational?

On one side, we have to admit that religion would be nothing without individuals to experience it (and experience it deeply and passionately); on the other, there's no religion without communities that come together and build it—in fact, there may be no heightened *individual* experience without some kind of group to foment it. Hence the dilemma: is religion to be found in the "feelings, acts, and experiences of individual[s] . . . in their solitude," as James would have it, or is it "eminently social," as Durkheim would claim? To take one step further, this chapter has also discussed a number of theorists who align the essence of religion with both the individual and non-rational experiences: James and Otto present clear examples of this move. Other figures, like Durkheim and Weber, see religion, society, and an ordered existence as closely linked.

Of course, such issues are never either/or, and all of the theorists we have discussed so far recognized that the opposites must somehow come together: in religions, shadows sometimes creep into the clearing, just as the campfire can penetrate the jungle. But in the task of interpretation, it is always a question of emphasis: in any given context, which perspective tells us more? The ideas you have studied so far are now ready for your testing and application—but the range of theoretical possibilities only opens wider in the next chapter.

Notes

[1]   Peter L. Berger, *The Sacred Canopy: Elements of a Sociological Theory of Religion* (New York: Doubleday, 1967), 23.

[2]   Rudolf Otto, *The Idea of the Holy*, trans. John W. Harvey (London, Oxford, and New York: Oxford University Press, 1958), 8.

[3]   *Ibid.*, 5.

[4]   *Ibid.*, 7.

[5]   *Ibid.*, 31.

[6]   *Ibid.*, 6.

[7]   *Ibid.*, 12–13.

[8]   William James, *The Varieties of Religious Experience: A Study in Human Nature* (New York: Penguin Books, 1987), 498.

[9]   *Ibid.*, 5.

[10]   *Ibid.*, 30.

[11]   *Ibid.*, 242.

[12]   *Ibid.*, 380–82.

[13] *Ibid.*, 31.
[14] Emile Durkheim, *The Elementary Forms of Religious Life*, trans. Joseph Ward Swain (New York: The Free Press, 1965), 52.
[15] *Ibid.*, 22.
[16] *Ibid.*, 15.
[17] *Ibid.*, 20.
[18] *Ibid.*, 123.
[19] *Ibid.*, 229.
[20] *Ibid.*, 236.
[21] *Ibid.*, 248.
[22] *Ibid.*, 62.
[23] Max Weber, *From Max Weber: Essays in Sociology*, trans. H.H. Gerth and C. Wright Mills (New York: Oxford University Press, 1958), 280.
[24] Max Weber, *The Protestant Ethic and the Spirit of Capitalism*, trans. Talcott Parsons (New York: Charles Scribner's Sons, 1958), 53.
[25] *Ibid.*, 181.
[26] Max Weber, *The Sociology of Religion*, trans. Ephraim Fischoff (Boston, MA: Beacon Press, 1991), 164.
[27] *Ibid.*, 46.
[28] *Ibid.*, 59.
[29] Weber, *From Max Weber*, 295.
[30] *Ibid.*, 281.
[31] *Ibid.*, 353.
[32] Arnold van Gennep, *The Rites of Passage*, trans. Monika B. Vizedom and Gabrielle L. Caffee (Chicago: University of Chicago Press, 1960), 10.
[33] *Ibid.*, 11.
[34] *Ibid.*, 191.
[35] *Ibid.*, 197.
[36] Victor Turner, *The Ritual Process: Structure and Anti-Structure* (Ithaca, NY: Cornell University Press, 1989), 95.
[37] Turner, *Dramas, Fields, and Metaphors*, 47.
[38] Turner, *The Ritual Process*, 95.
[39] Turner, *Dramas, Fields, and Metaphors*, 47.
[40] Turner, *The Ritual Process*, 126.
[41] *Ibid.*, 97.
[42] *Ibid.*, 128.
[43] *Ibid.*, 112.
[44] *Ibid.*, 138.
[45] *Ibid.*, 267.
[46] Clifford Geertz, *The Interpretation of Cultures* (New York: Basic Books, 1973), 89.
[47] *Ibid.*, 91.
[48] *Ibid.*, 94.
[49] *Ibid.*, 96–7.

50 *Ibid.*, 98–9.
51 *Ibid.*, 104.
52 *Ibid.*, 110.
53 *Ibid.*, 112.
54 *Ibid.*, 90.

4 Classic theories in the study of religion: Part 2

You might recall that the English word "theory" comes from an ancient Greek term, *theoria*, and Plato was one of its earliest champions. In *The Republic*, Plato describes what it's like to have this kind of vision in a fable called "the Allegory of the Cave." Recalling this story will help us chart a second set of theoretical ideas that range from intense criticism of religion on one side to theological affirmation of its theological nature on the other.

Plato envisions a group of men trapped in a dark cave. Chains bind them to the floor and force them to look only at the back wall. Behind them and at some distance, a fire burns, and between the men and the fire there is a partition, along which attendants carry various objects that cast shadowy projections. These are the only images that the chained men see, the only reality that they know. Now Plato imagines what would happen if one of the men somehow broke free, turned, saw the puppet show behind the reality he had perceived, and then made his way out of the cave. At first the light would be blinding, and the man would be disoriented. But then he would see the true world outside. What would happen, Plato wonders, if the man tried to return to the cave to educate his former comrades? Without a doubt, they would call him crazy, drive him away, and maybe even kill him.

In the classic Greek sense of the term, theory is "deep seeing," or seeing what truly is. So the escapee in Plato's story has gained theoretical vision of that which encompasses everything in the cave, and he tries to share his wisdom with the folks below. With regard to theory in the study of religion, this raises an interesting question: When it comes to religion, where does the truth reside? For some, religion itself *is* the illusion, the chains that keep people from seeing reality, and thus the proper theory of religion should liberate us from it. For others, religion emanates from outside the cave: our everyday world binds us to images and material things, and so theory must break these chains and lead us out to the (religious) truth.

We would need a philosopher to assist us in making a judgment about who is right in this debate, and that's not quite our job here.

But the fact is, both of these perspectives have something to offer in the interpretation of religion. Even the harshest critics of religion have contributed valuable insights, and a theologian's commitment to a particular faith does not necessarily rule his or her ideas out of bounds. As always, it is up to you to evaluate the theoretical ideas you read about, to think about and anticipate which ones might assist in understanding religious phenomena the best.

Is religion inside of the cave or out? That's hard to know, but whatever it is, Plato tells us that *theoria* frees the mind and improves our ability to see what's true. All the figures discussed below would likely agree on this foundational principle.

Religion as illusion

As the previous chapter indicated, the Enlightenment period had a tremendous impact on the way people looked at religion. You will recall that the philosopher Immanuel Kant laid down the challenge: "Dare to be wise." Kant was calling for humanity to grow up. For centuries, according to him, unquestioned beliefs and superstitions had dominated, but the time had come for human beings to think for themselves. Religion needed to be put on trial in the court of reason.

One of the most significant trends in the modern critique of religion emerged in German thought after Kant. G.W.F. *Hegel* (1770–1831), for example, took Kant's "dare to be wise" to the extreme: in one of his works, he claimed to have presented the thought of God before creation! This thought, or the "mind" (*Geist*) behind everything, provided the conceptual playbook for the way the world has unfolded, according to Hegel. Strangely enough, for "mind" to realize its plans, and for it to see and know itself, it had to try to view itself from the outside, to go outside itself and make itself concrete and particular, not just universal. It did just that in the material world and in humanity in particular, but at the same time this "mind" was *alienated* from itself. Humanity *is* that alienated part of *Geist*, a little bit of real self-knowledge, constantly running up against a world that does not seem to make sense at all, blocking it from coming home. But as Hegel attempted to show, throughout history the human intellect had gradually made progress in politics, the arts, philosophy, and, of course, in religion. Finally, in his day and age, Hegel claimed that *Geist* had arrived at itself again because a human mind (Hegel's) had understood it.

While Hegel's system scaled the heights of human reason, some critics highlighted its theological undertone. *Geist*, which Hegel associated with the mind of God, was at its center. *Ludwig Feuerbach* (1804–72) drew heavily on Hegel, but as a staunch humanist, Feuerbach reversed his scheme. In *The Essence of Christianity* (1841), Feuerbach argued that Hegel got it all wrong: it's not the divine "mind" that is alienated from itself in making humans; rather, the human "mind" is alienated from itself by making God. Religion begins in the conception of the infinite, which then takes on a life of its own: we allow ourselves to forget that *we* were the ones who conceived it. Feuerbach asserts that the infinite is in us, as human beings, in our potential, not "out there" as the essential quality of an object, God. But once the infinitely powerful object is set up, we give everything over to it: we project human qualities on God and thus renounce those qualities in ourselves (e.g., love, mercy, justice, power, etc.). We say, "It's all in God's hands," and as a consequence, this projected image, the illusion that is God and religion, causes human beings to swear off what is best in themselves. In response, Feuerbach recommended overcoming this illusion by recognizing that God and religion are of our own making.

Here you'll notice two concepts that become crucial in the modern critique of religion: *alienation* and *projection*. Modifying Hegel, Feuerbach proposed that religion is a force that alienates human beings from themselves, from their own true nature and potential. And in so doing, he suggested that the otherworldly forces that drive religion are of our own making: they are a projection of very human qualities and quandaries. In religious consciousness, illusions that we ourselves have constructed enthrall us, and Feuerbach called for them to be dispelled.

During the next century, a number of thinkers, including Karl Marx and Sigmund Freud, took this critique to its extreme.

Karl Marx

Karl Marx (1818–83) is of course famous for his opposition to capitalism and his founding of communism, but he also generated a highly influential theory of religion, one that has resonated in sociology and religious studies up to the present day.

Marx rejected the highly abstract philosophy of his era (like Hegel's) and promoted a *materialist* perspective that was designed to have *practical* implications for human existence. Turning away from the "rule of thoughts,"[1] Marx focused on "real individuals, their activity and the material conditions under which they live."[2] Humans are finite, biological entities who have a prodigious ability to produce and refashion nature. So the truth of human existence is on the ground, in the organization of labor, goods, and exchange. The point of uncovering this truth, according to Marx, is to make life better: "The philosophers have only *interpreted* the world ... the point is to *change* it."[3]

So if human nature is essentially biological and economic, where do our complex human institutions come from? What about our grand political, legal, moral, and philosophical principles? Marx's answer: from the "material life-process" itself. History is *really* the story of people putting food on the table, making sure they have a roof over their heads, and trying to reproduce both themselves and their wealth. Abstractions ("ideology" in Marx's terms) are a product of those arrangements: morality, religion, politics, and philosophy mirror the reality of history, the material conditions of our survival.

Because history is about these material conditions, it is also a story of inequality and conflict. From the earliest moments of social interaction, one individual or group commands the work of others, so there is a "division of labor": one person is assigned one particular job, one person does another, and so on—but the person in charge reaps most of the benefits. The most basic distinction, therefore, is the one between the property owners and the propertyless workers. As this distinction becomes more differentiated, it becomes the origin of *classes*, like aristocrats, the middle class, and workers. *Class struggle* is the engine of history for Marx and is that from which more abstract forms of human culture, like religion, arise.

To this extent, Marx agreed with Feuerbach that religion is a human product, and yet he identified its origins more precisely. As a general rule, Marx asserted that the situation for the vast majority of people throughout history had been miserable. Culminating in the modern, capitalist system, the owners of the *means of production* (the property, the labor, the factories, etc.) made more and more profit simply because they *owned*. This huge divide between the haves and the have-nots led to intense physical hardship for the masses. It also generated various forms of psychological *alienation*. For one thing, laborers were dehumanized by having their effort bought and sold, while fulfilling a social role that had been thrust upon them. In addition, a modern industrial laborer performed one repetitive action over and over again on an assembly line and never got to see the final product. Finally, the competition between laborers led to the unraveling of social bonds, except for those that served the interest of the owner.

From Marx's analytical perspective, the exploitation of the masses was transparent, and yet relatively few could see it. Why? The answer: *ideology*, and its worst form, *religion*. Like every abstract form of consciousness, Marx proposed, religion expresses the underlying material conditions that dominate in any given period, but its most essential function is to keep people from thinking about their situation. Thus "the criticism of religion is the premise of all criticism": religion is the essence of the illusions that keep human beings in bondage and servitude because it discourages analysis and critique in general. *So dispelling the illusion that is religion is the first step in dispelling them all.*[4]

This said, Marx was not entirely dismissive of religion because he claimed to understand its origins. He acknowledged that it expresses the impoverishment, suffering, exploitation, and alienation of the masses throughout history. Hence "[r]eligion is the sigh of the oppressed creature, the sentiment of a heartless world, and the soul of soulless conditions. It is the *opium* of the people."[5] To this extent, Marx found the persistence of religion understandable. For someone who is paid next to nothing to work under terrible conditions, commitment to the nobility of silent suffering, belief in an eternal soul that is different from the body, and hope for eternal life in another world after this one are principles that make a great deal of sense. While they are in fact illusions, they numb the pain of a profoundly difficult life.

And yet such beliefs are, in the end, false. Religion blinds the exploited laborer, so it can only serve the interests of those in charge: "The ideas of the ruling class are in every epoch the ruling ideas."[6] This means that religion expresses "the sigh of the oppressed," but at the same time it manipulates and controls. For example, from a Marxian perspective, it's good for the capitalist factory-owner if his workers adhere to basic Christian principles. Be humble. Follow the example of the suffering Christ. Purify yourself through work. Avoid wealth and material things. Suppress the needs and desires of the body. Think about your treasure laid up in heaven, not about this world. And so on. Only by shedding such ideological illusions could the workers see the reality of their situation and take action to improve it.

Despite his antipathy towards religion, it could be said that Marx had his own messianic, utopian vision of heaven on earth: he envisioned the division between the haves and the have-nots reaching a breaking point, and as a result, the workers would overthrow their masters in a massive global revolution and then institute a propertyless, classless society. This vision was highly idealistic, but, indeed, Marx's purpose was not to interpret the world but to change it.

Marx's critique of religion was designed to serve this agenda, and his theory does tend towards *reductionism*: religion is *solely* an illusory product of economic circumstances and constitutes nothing in particular by itself. Nevertheless, he was also a precursor for moderate and nuanced theories. Marx thought that any abstract form of human consciousness is itself a social product, which reminds us that we must see even the most elusive, esoteric expressions of religious commitment in the context of concrete, historical circumstances. As the discussion of figures like Durkheim and Weber has shown, applying this insight doesn't have to make us as antagonistic towards religion as Marx himself was.

Marx   *Religion as comfort*

The quote: "The basis of irreligious criticism is this: *man makes religion*; religion does not make man ... It is *the fantastic realization* of the human being inasmuch as the *human being* possesses no true reality ... Religious suffering is at the same time an *expression* of real suffering and a *protest* against real suffering. Religion is the sigh of the oppressed creature, the sentiment of a heartless world, and the soul of soulless conditions. It is the *opium* of the people."[7]

What to look for:

- The material conditions under which people live, and their effect on religious sensibilities and beliefs. Religion and work, class, money, property, and politics.
- Does participation in religion distract people from their economic circumstances? Does it serve to manipulate or cloud the minds of its adherents? Is it the "opium of the people"?
- The situation of both the oppressed and the ruling elite: Where does religion serve the interests of both of these groups?
- Religion as a product: the marketing and selling of religious objects, experiences, membership, etc.

Sigmund Freud

Like Karl Marx, Sigmund Freud has become a household name: his ideas, like "the ego," "the unconscious," and "the talking cure" (therapy), are now inextricably tied to the way we understand ourselves. And again, like Marx, Freud presented a theory of religion that aimed to expose its illusory nature. Its classic formulation appeared in the 1927 work, *The Future of an Illusion*.

Freud is most famous for his contributions to the psychology of the individual. Thanks to psychoanalytic theory, we now think of childhood as formative, particularly in structuring the libidinal drive, the in-born desire for pleasure and satisfaction. In Freud's classic account of childhood development, the mother is the first love-object for the child because she satisfies the child's needs and protects it. But later, the father steps in to perform this function. This intervention produces ambivalence: the child fears the father as a distant authority figure and perhaps even wants him out of the picture, but at the same time admires him. The make-up of the individual players in this drama, in addition to the potential interference of external events, will determine whether the child smoothly negotiates this *Oedipus complex*.

Most often a lot is left unsaid and suppressed in this drama: it happens to a child, who is by nature a passive participant. And yet he or she still has instincts and desires, and when they are suppressed, these feelings become the sub-conscious forces at work in adult behaviors, moods, and emotions—forces that are not always easy to acknowledge. Instead, they appear, often garbled by the transition from the unconscious to the conscious mind, in dreams, in slips of the tongue, and in misdirected obsessions and attachments. If the sub-merged "baggage" is too much, producing harmful symptoms that keep a patient from living a happy life, Freud devised a cure: talking to a therapist, who would guide him or her in unraveling the problem. Then the "rational operation of the intellect" might replace "the effects of repression";[8] i.e., one can live and think for oneself.

In *Future of an Illusion*, Freud generalizes this theory and applies it to "civilization." In fact, civilized society grows like a self, and for it to function, basic instincts need to be kept in check or properly channeled. But the problem is, according to Freud, that people still have them. So what do we do? The answer: we must receive some return on suppressing our true desires. No one really likes to sacrifice instant gratification in favor of hard work, for example, but society encourages this behavior and bestows "mental assets" as compensation: one may be forced to work 12-hour days to make ends meet, but one can always take pride in being "the salt of the earth," or maybe even better yet, being an American citizen, who has a "share in the task of ruling other nations and dictating their laws."[9] Like Marx, Freud believed that such abstractions both expressed and masked real conditions of human existence. But Freud emphasized the *libidinal* part of our nature, perhaps explaining why certain "mental assets" have appeal: we want what we want, so for an idea to distract us from our desires, it *must* be *intensely* satisfying as a compensation.

But the cultural ideals of our civilization, like being a good citizen, a good wife or husband, a solid worker, proud soldier, etc. can only do so much. When confronted with the broader forces of the universe, particularly the overwhelming forces of nature and death, "the work of civilization" is not quite enough.[10] Our fear requires something even more soothing: the imagined presence of the gods. Freud argues that the gods are a collective representation of our individual experience as children. Deep down, he suggests, each of us knows the experience of fear and dependence because of the anxieties associated with being a child. When it comes to cosmic anxieties, we need BIG parents; we call out to divine presences for help; and we conceive them to care for us, but they can also be quite fearsome. This projection of individual experience onto a collective representation becomes most clear in Western monotheism, according to Freud, where polytheism gave way to the dominion of the one true God— the *Father* God.

The imaging of the Hebrew God as a scary but simultaneously benevolent father is a tip-off to Freud that this belief is a projection, and it is representative: religion in general is associated with staving off fear, weakness, and frailty, so the imagining of a powerful father-figure who controls nature and promises an overcoming of death makes a great deal of sense. This idea—and others like it—provide a powerful fulfillment of our wish to be free from helplessness, like the helplessness that afflicts a child. Religious notions also provide a satisfying compensation for whatever has gone wrong in our life: even if everything has fallen apart, there is still the gods/God to please and rely upon, with the promise of a better life after this one, in the comforting embrace of the divine.

Much of Freud's critique relies on a basic presupposition: religious beliefs cannot be empirically proven, and thus they are not rational. No one can prove, for example, that there is an immortal soul or a God. Therefore, religion is an *illusion*. So what is to be done about it? Even Freud acknowledged that "[r]eligion has clearly performed great services for human civilization. It has contributed much towards the taming of the asocial instincts."[11] But in keeping with his overarching theory, Freud notes that the continuing search for and obsession with imagined substitute parent figures—not to mention sexual prudery, which is a common mark of the religious sensibility—are signs of someone who "is destined to remain a child for ever, [who] can never do without protection against strange superior powers."[12] Just like the individual, the civilization that maintains an illusory basis for its cultural ideals and moral precepts needs therapy, the rational analysis of the scientific observer, in order to grow up and out of its childishness.

It should be noted that *Future of an Illusion* does not exhaust Freud's reflections on religion: he also commented extensively on totemism, fetishism, and the monotheistic traditions of the West. In addition, he was fascinated by ritual, and in an essay entitled "Obsessive Actions and Religious Practices," Freud explored the connections between what we would now call obsessive–compulsive behavior and religious rituals. While they are not the same, Freud suggested that both are the expression of repressed desires, often of a sexual nature. More importantly, Freud drew attention to the way in which religious practice tends to transform seemingly meaningless gestures or otherwise insignificant details into matters of great significance. Religion in this sense is a focusing lens, diverting attention from basic instincts to ritual attachments.

Thus we can see one way in which Freud's theoretical ideas, while entirely designed to undermine religion, still might contribute to a more balanced approach. Freud used a metaphor for religion that was reminiscent of Marx's "opium of the people": religion is the "sweet— or bitter-sweet—poison."[13] Nevertheless, Freud opened a whole new vista by linking individual psychology—particularly the psychology of human desire—with religious commitment. Religion may indeed be about the remarkable transformation of the small, the intimate, and the erotic into a grandiose projection on a very large screen.

Freud

The quote: "Religion would thus be the universal obsessional neurosis of humanity; like the obsessional neurosis of children, it arose out of the Oedipus complex, out of the relation to the father. If this view is right, it is to be supposed that a turning-away from religion is bound to occur with the fatal inevitability of a process of growth, and that we find ourselves at this very juncture in the middle of that phase of development."[14]

What to look for:

- The expression of libidinal, sexual, and/or bodily desires in religious contexts.
- The mirroring of family dynamics in religious symbols and doctrines.
- The connection between individual, psychological history and religious commitment: religion as "wish-fulfillment."
- Obsession in religious contexts, either with doctrines or ritual objects and activities.

Phenomenology of religion: Symbols, patterns, and dimensions

Carl Jung

To make the transition between psychoanalysis and the phenomeno-logical approach to the study of religion, we turn to Carl Jung (1875–1961). Jung was a collaborator with Freud until the two parted ways because of disagreements about the nature of psychoanalysis. Jung also resisted Freud's criticism of religion and invoked *phenomenological method* to generate a more sympathetic account.

We have already discussed phenomenological method in earlier chapters. You will recall that this approach recommends *bracketing* our usual view of the world before studying something. That leaves us open to the *phenomena* as they truly appear, allowing us to observe and describe them without prejudice. In *Psychology and Religion* (1937), Jung rejected the Freudian agenda and claimed that his approach is "exclusively phenomenological, that is, it is concerned with occur-rences, events, experiences, in a word, with facts. Its truth is a fact and not a judgment."[15] Jung goes on to use belief in "virgin birth" as an example: the point for a psychologist is not to determine whether it can really happen or not; instead, the mere fact that people have the belief is all that matters. You will notice that this perspective differs radically from both Marx and Freud, whose analyses were designed to expose such views as false.

But Jung did agree with Freud on many points, including the importance of the unconscious. Freud had already shown that the unconscious was a deep well of desires that had often been suppressed. Then, at some later point, they returned, and Freud mined obsessions, slips, dreams, and associations to discern what the subconscious was trying to say. *Symbols*, therefore, had to be at the center of psycho-analysis: if a patient had an irrational fear of dogs, for example, it was likely because dogs *symbolized* something in that person's background.

Of course religions are rife with symbols, and we know that Freud interpreted them as the product of psychosexual development. So, for example, when interpreting Leonardo da Vinci's "Virgin and Child with St. Anne," a painting that depicts the two women doting over the Christ-toddler, Freud focused on the fact that Leonardo himself was an illegitimate child: he had two mothers from whom he wanted attention (his birth-mother and his father's wife), a wish symbolized in the painting. In a broader sense, the painting reflects both an infantile desire for maternal attention and an anxiety about who one's real mother is: by consorting with the father, she proves her infidelity to the child! This is the Freudian approach: because they plug into patterns of individual neurosis, religious symbols acquire power and sustain themselves.

Jung agreed that the symbols are wrapped up in the unconscious, but instead of presenting them as garbled symptoms of unconscious dilemmas, he suggested that they transmitted a universal wisdom that eluded the conscious mind. The unconscious, in fact, is the "source of all life," not only because it harbors the drives Freud had discussed, but also because it contains "the creative seeds of the future and the roots of all constructive fantasies."[16] In encountering the contents of their own psyche, human beings are overwhelmed by its power, attribute its products to a divine source, and project them onto the world. So, for example, the sun becomes a god because it is emblematic of basic human experiences like life and death (sunrise and sunset), or our capacities, like wisdom and discernment ("shedding light on things"). To this extent, Jung agreed with the projection theory of Feuerbach, but unlike Marx and Freud, these kinds of projections are positive: they provide the gateway to primordial knowledge stored in the unconscious.

When it comes to the symbols we find in dreams, visions, art, and myths—symbols that intersect with what we call religion—Jung urged careful attention because they express the universal patterns of the human psyche. Jung called these patterns *archetypes*, "forms or images of a collective nature which occur practically all over the earth as constituents of myths and at the same time as ... individual products of unconscious origin."[17] Archetypes are the basic building blocks of meaning. They can be shapes, like circles or triangles, or numbers, likes pairs, threes, fours, or tens, but they are often less abstract, like the mother or father figure, the old sage or the child, the masculine and the feminine, the hero or the savior. In each case, the archetype points to a "metaphysical" reality, a truth that "transcends consciousness" and remains "unknowable as such," and this is the Jungian essence of religion.[18]

At the same time, these archetypes represent the accumulated wisdom of humankind, tried and true ways of bestowing meaning and order on human existence. As elements of a body of common, accumulated wisdom, Jung claims that archetypes come from a *collective unconscious*. Even though the symbols representing archetypes may be different, depending on the cultural or historical setting, the "analogy" and "sometimes even identity" between them can only arise from a common structure that all human beings share.[19] According to Jung's best guess, archetypes have become part of the permanent structure of our mind, having been passed down from generation to generation, almost like our genes.

So in the example discussed above, da Vinci's painting, Freud finds only the traces of Leonardo's biography. In contrast, Jung finds an expression of a universal archetype: the motif of the dual mother or dual descent, which leads to notion of being "twice-born." It is common to find figures in mythology who have both human and divine origins, or who undergo a transition that entails being "adopted" by a second mother. Jung cites the baptism of Jesus as an example, and his disciples follow this precedent and draw upon the same archetypal pattern.[20] Thus the artist had delved into the collective unconscious and expressed a fundamental human desire for transformation and rebirth.

This is not to say that Jung's theory of religion focuses entirely on its "collective" component. In fact, like Otto and James before him, Jung recommended that we emphasize "the original religious experience"[21] of the individual, as opposed to the texts, doctrines, practices, and institutions to which it has given rise. It's just that the meaning of the experience of the "individual" has changed for modern people. The mythic, religious person of yesteryear could only say that "something thinks in him" because "[t]he spontaneity of the act of thinking does not lie, causally, in his conscious mind, but in his unconscious."[22] Since the archetypes "thought in him," the "primitive" was in touch with the profound workings of the universal human drama. Collective symbols, myth, and ritual provided the "mental therapy for the sufferings of mankind, such as hunger, war, disease, old age, and death."[23]

Under the tutelage of figures like Freud, in contrast, the modern individual seeks a different form of therapy: rational detachment from both the unconscious and the collective. Mythic thinking still persists in vestigial form (Jung wrote an interesting treatise on UFOs, which he calls a "modern myth," to prove his point), but by distancing themselves from the archetypal unconscious, modern people had cut themselves off from the collective source of life and creativity, "the lower stories of the skyscraper of rational consciousness." So the job of the Jungian therapist is to make that connection once again, or else we nervously suspend the psyche in mid-air.[24] What else is therapy, Jung reasoned, than the creation of a personal myth, one in which the patient could get in touch with powerful symbols and become a hero or heroine—a savior to oneself? And what else is "linking back" to these archetypes but the essence of *re-ligio*?[25]

We should note that Jung's ideas, while themselves well known, have become even more famous in the hands of *Joseph Campbell* (1904–87). In books such as *The Hero with a Thousand Faces*, *The Masks of God*, and *The Power of Myth*, Campbell reiterated many of

Jung's ideas for a popular audience, with an emphasis on the universal commonality of basic motifs in religious traditions the world over. Scholars have questioned this kind of analysis for its tendency to override differences in favor of similarities: just because both Jesus and the Buddha were hero/saviors, does that mean the meaning of these two figures is the same for their followers? Just because many great religious pilgrimages share similar elements, does that mean they are all the same journey?

But an even bigger question arises out of this consideration of the Jungian approach in the study of religion. While figures like Freud and Marx can be accused of *reductionism*, that is, transforming religion into something that is *truly* and *solely* economic or psychosexual in nature, Jung can be found guilty of doing the exact opposite: his theory posits some universal something, some inaccessible *je ne sais quoi*, which is the true essence of religion. While one approach might be too simplistic, the other sounds a lot like a theological defense: the truth behind religion is a uniquely religious thing that is beyond the human capacity to know or analyze it. Sounds a lot like . . . God. In any event, if the agenda behind the Jungian theory is to defend myth and religion, then it violates the *phenomenological* principles with which he, and we, began.

Jung

The quote: "Religion appears to me to be a peculiar attitude of the human mind, which could be formulated in accordance with the original use of the term 'religio,' that is, a careful consideration and observation of certain dynamic factors, understood to be 'powers,' spirits, demons, gods, laws, ideas, ideals or whatever name man has given to such factors as he has found in his world powerful, dangerous or helpful enough to be taken into careful consideration, or grand, beautiful and meaningful enough to be devoutly adored and loved."[26]

What to look for:

- The role of preconscious, pre-rational dreams, myths, and visions in religious life.
- Universal motifs or *archetypes* expressed by symbols in different religious traditions: shapes, numbers, or figures of the masculine and the feminine, the child, the old person, the hero/savior, etc.

- The therapeutic function of religion, especially by means of its myths and symbols.
- The persistence of symbols, myths, and archetypes in modern life (i.e., in dreams, politics, popular culture, etc.).

Mircea Eliade

Mircea Eliade (1907–86), a Romanian-born scholar who spent much of his career teaching at the University of Chicago, was one of the true founders of the modern study of religion. While his theories have been controversial in recent years, in part because some scholars see in them a veiled theological defense of religion like Jung's, they are important touchstones for any beginner in the field.

In one of his most representative works, *The Sacred and the Profane: The Nature of Religion* (1959), Eliade asserts that the essence of religious life is an encounter with the *sacred*, and he aims to open up the "*sacred in its entirety*," in all the ways it appears.[27] To this extent, *The Sacred and the Profane* epitomizes Eliade's broad, *phenomenological* approach to the history of religions.

Eliade begins with some basic assumptions. In keeping with Durkheim, the first thing to say about the sacred is that it is *not* the *profane*; it is that which is set aside or different from our everyday, mundane experience. Second, the sacred doesn't just sit there; we tend to know and experience it because it "*shows itself to us.*" Eliade calls this "*act of the manifestation* of the sacred" a *hierophany*, literally an "appearance of the sacred/holy."[28] Perhaps the most famous example of a *hierophany* in the Western tradition is the appearance of the burning bush to Moses: in this story the sacred breaks into the world through a natural object, which is a common occurrence in archaic religion. According to Eliade, an episode like this is powerful because it shows that there is a higher *power* and *reality*. Profane existence is characterized by sameness and routine, but the religious person is sensitive to the sacred because it is "really real," as opposed to the banality of the everyday. In fact, "Religious man [*homo religiosus*] thirsts for *being*," Eliade argues, and only the sacred can quench that thirst.[29]

In Eliade's work, the human response to the sacred generally takes three forms that are themselves intimately tied together: *symbol, myth, and ritual.*

Symbol: As the discussion of Freud and Jung indicated, a symbol is something that stands in for something else. A tree in the backyard of your childhood home, for example, might symbolize being innocent and carefree, evoking good memories. But religious symbols are distinctive, according to Eliade, because they make the world of the sacred appear, and they do so in a universal sense. So each individual tree refers to a great mythical tree that holds the whole cosmos together, including the underworld in its roots and the heavens in its branches. Thus each tree has a sacred quality, because each refers to the sense of order and harmony provided by the original.

Myth: Like Jung, Eliade thought that myth was the most fundamental stratum of religious life. The key point about myths is that they convey "a primordial event that took place at the beginning of time."[30] All myths could, in a sense, begin with "Once upon a time ..." because they relate events that occurred in some ancient, sacred past, close to the beginning of the world. They often have to do with creation, sometimes with creation of the universe or human beings, other times with the origins of objects or things we find valuable, powerful, or intriguing. They also provide the paradigm for human behavior. The religious person, according to Eliade, is immersed in these models and does little in life without mythic precedent: everything must be done in accordance with what the primordial gods and heroes did in the beginning.

Ritual: If myths provide the stories that recapture the sacred origin, then ritual is the conscious, repeated act of following its precedents. Sometimes mere mortals can *literally* do what the great gods and heroes did in their myths; often they cannot. In either case, the features of the ritual take on a *symbolic* significance. For example, a god or hero might have killed a "marine monster" and "dismembered its body in order to create the cosmos." Now, to consecrate a new beginning of some sort (building a house/temple, starting a journey, beginning a new stage of life, and so on), the religious person might make a sacrifice, symbolically killing the monster, to recapture and "actualize" the sacred beginning once again.[31]

By means of these three functions, the sacred and its appearances come to provide an organizing principle for human life. We can see that particularly well when we think about the ways in which the sacred manifests itself in both *space* and *time*. For example, "[S]pace," Eliade argues, "is not homogeneous": it has "breaks in it; some parts of space are qualitatively different from others."[32] This point is easy to grasp: certain places have an aura around them that marks them off from the everyday, places like the Grand Canyon or the Ground Zero site in Lower Manhattan. Sacred spaces, in a religious sense, have a similar aura, but they also recall the founding of a new world and thus provide a "central axis for all future orientation."[33] Instead of wandering aimlessly, the devotee has an orienting point around which his or her spatial life is organized.

This orienting center is often thought to be a pole, a pillar, a mountain, a tree, and so on, or, of course, it could be a building that marks the spot where an original hierophany took place. Such structures symbolize an axis of the world (an *axis mundi*), a vertical center. But the influence of an orienting axis spreads outward as well: the original center radiates its sacrality to outposts (e.g. temples or churches) that are at the center of their own local realms. In fact, this analogy can be taken further. In traditional religious settings, the home itself is an organizing center, and it takes on a special symbolic value, distinguishing it from the world outside. The last step in this "system of micro-macrocosmic correspondences"[34] might be a room, or even the body. Have you ever thought about how your room is, in a sense, your sacred space? And perhaps you have heard the people say that "the body is a temple"?

In each of these cases, from the macro- to the micro, rituals surround the sacred center. Eliade discusses rituals that must be performed before crossing the threshold of a space, for example, and those that accompany the building of a house or a new temple. Mythic stories naturally accompany these ritual gestures. So if building a house or a local temple is like creating a new world by imposing order on a chaotic world, then it would correspond with an ancient story about the way the world was founded, like the example of the sacrifice of the primordial beast, discussed above.

Time is the other mode through which the sacred makes itself known. Eliade asserts that "like space," time "is neither homogeneous nor continuous."[35] That is, some days or periods are marked off as special, like a birthday, New Year's Day, or even Spring Break. But, again, Eliade claims that sacred time has a distinct quality. In contrast with the ceaseless progress of moments and days and months and years in everyday, profane time, sacred time always refers back to "that time" (*illud tempus*) when the world was founded and the gods performed their legendary deeds. To this extent, when a religious person enters sacred time, it is like becoming time*less*. Especially for "archaic man," sacred time is cyclical and "reversible" because it circles back to an "eternal mythical present"[36] that can always be brought back through symbol, myth, and ritual.

So how do religious people perform this remarkable act of time travel? Times are first and foremost symbolic, so a day that is just like any other for someone else might be significant for you, like a birthday. When it comes to religious holidays and festivals, the symbolism goes deeper, so the New Year, to take one example, always refers to the *creation* or *recreation* of the world, thus linking it with the sacred. Obviously the symbolic power of a holy time is therefore related to *myth*. A story of creation gives the content to the sense of renewal and new beginnings, and often these myths are recited during New Year's celebrations. As we have already discovered, evoking the *experience* of the sacred is the job of *ritual*. Often religious traditions will invite some measure of ritual chaos on the night before New Year's, allowing an opportunity for the playing out of the old. Then, when the new day dawns, order is re-imposed by invoking the mythic precedents for the creation of the world—and the community can start with a clean slate.

It should be noted that Eliade's theories led him to make a number of controversial distinctions. For example, he isolated Judaism and Christianity because they rely on a sense of linear, irreversible time, as opposed to the cyclical concept present in many other traditions. In addition, Eliade conceived the sacred and the profane as "two modes of being in the world, two existential situations assumed by man in the course of his history."[37] For *homo religiosus*, the sacred was always with him, always within reach and at the center of his life. But modern, profane individuals have no such center: their time is linear and monotonous; their space is homogeneous, bland, and neutral. While vestiges of the sacred remain, moderns are generally lost because they no longer have a deep religious sensibility.

As Walter Capps argued, Eliade's phenomenology was designed to recapture precisely this sense: to rediscover the sacred and open up this part of our consciousness once again. To this extent, Eliade's theory was intended to have "an important religious function."[38] This means that like Jung, Eliade seemingly had an agenda in putting forth his phenomenology of religion, one that relied about a prior commitment to the *reality* of the sacred. Does this mean, in the end, that he failed to follow phenomenological guidelines, or that his version of phenomenology led to limited results? This challenge is potent, and yet Eliade's analysis remains valuable, especially for the beginning student of religion.

Eliade

The quote: "Whatever the historical context in which he is placed, *homo religiosus* always believes that there is an absolute reality, *the sacred*, which transcends this world but manifests itself in this world, thereby sanctifying it and making it real. He further believes that life has a sacred origin and that human existence realizes all of its potentialities in proportion as it is religious—that is, participates in reality. The gods created man and the world, the culture heroes completed the Creation, and the history of all these divine and semidivine works is preserved in myths. By reactualizing sacred history, by imitating the divine behavior, man puts and keeps himself close to the gods—that is, in the real and the significant."[39]

What to look for:

- Manifestations of the sacred (hierophanies) in space and time. Space: the feeling of sacred space, rituals surrounding it, the *axis mundi* ("center of the world"). Time: reversible, repeatable time; *illud tempus, in illo tempore* ("that time," "in that time," i.e., time at the beginning of the world); the "eternal present" of sacred time.
- Mapping the sacred in terms of symbol, myth, and ritual. Symbols reveal a "more real" world behind this one. Myths refer to *illud tempus* ("that time") and set precedents for religious people. Rituals reactualize myths and allow repeated experience of the sacred.
- Universal patterns and motifs of religious life (e.g., trees, stones, fruit, mountains, water, the sun, the moon, buildings, animals, etc.).
- Vestiges of the sacred in contemporary life and human psychology.

Ninian Smart

A relatively contemporary version of phenomenological method comes to us from *Ninian Smart* (1927–2001), a Scottish philosopher of religion who spent much of his career teaching at the University of Lancaster in England and at the University of California-Santa Barbara. Smart's body of work spanned the full, global range of philosophical, religious, and secular worldviews.

This term "worldview" is vital in Smart's theory of religion because it helps put things in perspective. Philosophers (like the Greeks, or Confucius) managed to construct coherent and complete systems for living the good life, and the modern era has given rise to a number of secular visions of the world that offer a thorough account of it (like Marxism, or nationalism). So Smart was not prepared to say that religion was the only comprehensive way for human beings to construct order and meaning: analysis of religion is but one aspect of "worldview analysis."[40]

But it is a big one. Smart's basic premise is that studying religion is about discovering "the various ways in which human beings conceive of themselves, and act in the world."[41] To achieve this goal, according to Smart, we must apply a version of the phenomenological method. Once again, the starting point is *bracketing*, the suspension of both one's own beliefs and judgments about whether the worldview of another is true or false. But Smart is famous for emphasizing a further step: to study religion requires a special form of imagination, the *empathetic imagination*, which "tries to bring out what religious acts mean to the actors."[42] From Chapter 1, you might recall the image that was one of Smart's favorites: the empathetic imagination allows us to find out what it's like to walk a mile in another person's moccasins.[43]

This metaphor can be misleading: it does not suggest that the study of religion is about a personal communion with the experience of others (i.e., "sharing"). In fact, *scholarly empathy requires comparative analysis of the religious worldview in all of its dimensions*. Like Eliade, Smart attempted to discern patterns in religious life by absorbing the data and then comparing it across the boundaries of cultures and traditions. But in contrast to Eliade, Smart did not insist on tying these patterns down to a single definition or essence (i.e., the *reality* of the *sacred*). Instead, he avoided definition and let the patterns, or *dimensions* of religious worldviews speak for themselves: taken together, they "give a kind of functional delineation of religions in lieu of a strict definition."[44]

We turn now to the seven dimensions of religion that Smart identified. As you survey Smart's categories, you should think about examples from your own knowledge of religious worldviews:

The ritual or practical dimension. Religion "involves such activities as worship, meditation, pilgrimage, sacrifice, sacramental rites and healing activities."[45] Worship, contemplation, transformation, and social practices are crucial aspects of the ritual dimension. Examples: prayer, singing, dancing, chanting, recitation, meditation, pilgrimage, bathing/washing, linguistic/social practices, etc.

The doctrinal or philosophical dimension. Religious traditions often emphasize standard sets of belief and/or forms of analysis meant to critique and support them. Examples: adherence to basic doctrines, like belief in the existence of a God/gods, the truth of a body of scriptures, or a certain picture of the cosmos; theological and/or philosophical traditions that debate and bolster these doctrines.

The mythic or narrative dimension. "Every religion has its stories."[46] Narrative is synonymous with memory for Smart, and it confers a sense of identity for both individuals and groups. Mythic narratives also provide the basis for both ritual and sacred space, and articulate both origins and the end of the cosmic story, as we found in Eliade.[47] Examples: stories of creation, the gods, early heroes, a religion's founder, great luminaries in the tradition, personal testimonials, the afterlife, or the end of the world.

The experiential and emotional dimension. "[W]e are creatures of flesh and blood, and death, sex, fear, love, pleasure, and so forth" are crucial elements in the religious life.[48] But religious experience also stretches out to the calmer, contemplative side. Examples: expression of emotions in religious contexts, like fear, sadness, bliss, or compassion; ecstatic, mystical, and/or contemplative experience.

The ethical or legal dimension. What is the right thing to do? All religious traditions have something to say about this question, often codifying their responses in public morality or a body of law. Examples: scriptural bodies of religious law, or bodies of law based on scripture; codes of conduct ordained for religious communities to guide their religious and social practices.

The organizational or social dimension. All religions have leaders and representatives who belong to institutions that are committed to the work of sustaining the tradition. Examples: pastors, priests, gurus, rabbis, imams, shamans, theologians, lawyers, etc., and the institutions to which they belong; intersection between religious and political leadership.

The material or artistic dimension. Finally, "A religion or worldview will express itself typically in material creations, from chapels to cathedrals to temples to mosques, from icons and divine statuary to books and pulpits."[49]

As you can see, Smart's dimensions provide us with a remarkable framework for describing religious worldviews. For one thing, they aid in making comparisons across the boundaries of different religions: How does one tradition compare with another when it comes to each of these dimensions? These categories also assist in comparing between religious worldviews and non-religious worldviews. How would a secular worldview express these components as compared to a religious worldview? Where might the two overlap?

But we should also think about the work these categories do in describing what's going on *within* a broader religious worldview. "Christianity," for example, is not just one thing, so it's useful to engage in dimensional comparison of different branches and communities within it: How might a Lutheran community in Minnesota compare to a Southern Baptist congregation when it comes to the experiential or emotional component of the Christian worldview? How do the Eastern Orthodox, Catholic, and Protestant branches differ on the matter of doctrine and belief? And so on.

Smart also emphasizes the dynamic interplay of these dimensions within worldviews.[50] In reading the summary presented above, you undoubtedly made connections: Doesn't a ritual often depend on mythic precedents? And doesn't the ritual evoke some deep emotional and experiential responses? And isn't it related to the central beliefs and doctrines of a worldview? And what about all of the trappings of a ritual, all the material and aesthetic objects? Who leads the ritual, and what kind of social connections are forged? And is a ritual encouraged within the tradition to reinforce certain ideas about right and wrong? By examining the way the different dimensions interact with each other, Smart proposes that his theory is not just a typology: it also gives us a way to account for change and development within a religious community's worldview. Change through time is the product of the shifting relationships between these different elements.

As useful as it is, not all observers are thrilled with Smart's version of phenomenology. The call for empathetic imagination, for example, still seems to hand over considerable authority to the insider, calling to mind the dilemma discussed in Chapter 2. Do we really have to see the world the way the insider sees it to understand his or her religious tradition? And who will decide whether we have really walked in his or her moccasins or not? Wouldn't that have to be the insider him- or herself? Nevertheless, Smart relied on the comparative and dimensional approach itself to respond to such objections. The insider will rarely have broad perspective, and thus it's even plausible for the student of religion to correct him or her.[51] While critics have debated to this defense, there's no doubt that Smart's phenomenology of religion frees itself from theological premises, those maintained by so many theorists before him.

Smart

The quotes: "The history of religions ... involves depicting histories, but in a manner which involves empathy ... [It] is delicate and has a sensitive soul ... a distancing, and yet a warmth; objectivity and yet subjectivity of spirit; description but also evocation; method, but also imagination."[52]

"From history and from comparative study of religions we can begin to piece together the so-to-say logical structure of systems— how the differing dimensions of religion ... are bound to one another in relations of implication and suggestion, of expression and definition; also, too, how within the range of doctrines in a system they are mutually related and organically influence one another."[53]

What to look for:

- Religion as a worldview alongside others, e.g., philosophical or secular/political visions.
- The opportunity to engage the religious worldview using the *empathetic imagination*: what would it be like to walk a mile in another person's shoes?
- Comparison between and within religious worldviews drawing on seven dimensions: ritual, doctrinal, mythic, experiential, ethical, institutional, material.

Back to theology?

As you have already discovered, the academic study of religion has its roots in the Enlightenment effort to prioritize rational, scholarly analysis over faith-based commitments. This legacy has led to a distinction between the perspective of the religious insider and the viewpoint of the religious studies scholar. The discussion in Chapter 2 captured this divide by describing several *Orders of Meaning* in the study of religion: the First Order, the *immediate*, is constituted by what insiders do, say, and feel while they are in the thick of things religiously; the Second Order, the *reflective*, is the level of insider reflection on the immediate, and theology is one of its components; and the Third Order is that of the *academic* outsider: the theories we have been investigating by and large participate in this level of analysis. But as we have seen, often things aren't so cut and dried. We have noticed places where theology (the Second Order of Meaning) seems to creep into the theories that have been so formative in constituting the field: this is probably because the contemporary study of religion owes as much to Christian theology as it does to Enlightenment critique.

Now we have to add yet another wrinkle: some forms of Christian theology adjusted to accommodate both post-Enlightenment ideas and the plurality of religious traditions that has come to light so vividly in the last two centuries. Some "orthodox" or "fundamentalist" theologians have wanted little to do with the study of religion,[54] but others felt the impact of both modern, non-religious thought *and* the insights that the study of religion produced. In response, they generated theories of religion that were born of theology but have become influential in the field as a whole. There's no better example of this phenomenon than Paul Tillich.

Paul Tillich

Paul Tillich (1886–1965) was a German theologian who left his homeland before the Second World War and came to the United States. He held teaching posts at Union Theological Seminary, Harvard Divinity School, and the University of Chicago, but also reached large audiences through his popular books and public lectures. His own brand of *existentialism* was decisively Christian, but it also lent itself to other traditions because religion in general, Tillich suggested, is a matter of being grasped by an *ultimate concern*.

First we need to consider *existentialism*. You will recall that the concept of *alienation* was decisive for figures like Hegel, Feuerbach, and Marx. Existentialists built on this idea: the first thing we can say about ourselves is that we *are*, that we exist in the world. Next we have to acknowledge that we are finite, that we are going to die. In the face of these circumstances, we are faced with an urgent decision. How are we going to *be*? What projects are we going to set for ourselves, knowing that our time is limited? This situation causes us anxiety because our decision can seem so arbitrary. Often it seems to be the product of external forces (our parents, our society, our friends, etc.). Then we think, "Why this option and not the others?" Every action we undertake excludes an infinite number of other possibilities. Maybe we manage to stand up to this horrible freedom and make a resolute choice ... and in the end we die. So isn't it all meaningless?

These questions are not cheery, and many existentialist thinkers seemed to give us no exit. Most of the ways people try to respond to these challenges, they claimed, are purely escapist: they get wrapped up in their lives, distract themselves through entertainment and chatter, and devise their various life projects, all the while remaining in denial of their finite existence. But the prime culprit is religion. Here you can see the connection between *projection theory*, discussed above, and existentialism. In the latter, religion is an attempt to escape both the responsibility of choosing a way of being and the inevitability of death. Christianity, for example, comforts us by telling us what kind of beings we are and dictating how we should behave in order to escape death. But according to the secular existentialist, none of its answers honestly addresses the situation that we are in.

Figures like Tillich opened themselves up to this challenge but thought differently about the status of religion. *Christian* existentialism sees the ideas described above as components of a powerful question, but religion, and Christianity in particular, does in fact provide an answer. Tillich affirmed that humankind suffers from a "tragic estrangement from [its] true being" that causes a spiritual "emergency."[55] He also agreed with the secular, philosophical existentialists that a lot of what generally counts as religion—indeed, a lot of what often counts as living a fulfilling life—does not actually speak to our existential situation. For the most part we are occupied with what Tillich calls "preliminary concerns," which include the trivial aspects of everyday existence, the individual concerns that seem somewhat more important (like exams, degrees, jobs, money, romance, etc.), and even the grander occupation of humankind (art, science, or politics).[56] Even religious people often get hung up on preliminaries: they suppose that everything religious hinges on the intellect, action, or emotion.[57] Or maybe they get absorbed by politics within the church, temple, or synagogue. Perhaps they go through the motions during rituals, recite scripture memorized by rote, or get fixated on a holy object while forgetting what's supposed to be behind it. Fleeing into the world of preliminary concerns is a constant enticement, given our existential situation.

In contrast, the essence of religion is an "ultimate concern": it is "independent of any conditions of character, desire, or circumstance"; it is "total," inescapable, and "infinite"; and "no moment or relaxation and rest is possible in the face of a religious concern which is ultimate, unconditional, total, and infinite."[58] The core of religious life is an absolute commitment, but it is not about an escape, as the secular existentialist would suggest. In fact, in the face of a world that constantly threatens us with death and meaninglessness, taking on an ultimate concern is the ultimate risk: it takes courage to concern oneself not solely with the preliminary things of this world, but primarily with something unconditional, total, and absolute. In other words, taking on an ultimate concern is a leap of faith—but it's an *existential* leap of faith, the only truly authentic decision about how one is going to be in the world.

Of course, Tillich argues, this concern is about *something* in particular: in his theology this something is called "the ground of Being," "*that which determines our being or not-being.*"[59] This unconditioned content of religious concern eludes human concepts or representation but is generally associated with "God." Tillich also tells us that his main purpose as a Christian theologian is to affirm the "New Being," Jesus Christ. Nevertheless, if we expand Tillich's ideas, as he himself did later in his life, the name we use for the object of religious concern is irrelevant, and its content may vary, as long as it is in fact *ultimate* ("unconditional, total, and infinite") for those who have it. To this extent, it is possible to identify ultimate concern in any worldview worth its salt—and this is the way Tillich's theological concept transmutes into a theory of religion in general.

To illustrate this transformation from theology to theory, you might think about "ultimate concern" as follows: ask yourself, why are you reading this book?[60] One possibility is that you are doing so simply because you have to, because it was assigned for a class. In that case, your concern is preliminary because it is related to a limited goal within the educational system. Perhaps your answer is "I am curious about the study of religion, what it does and where it came from." That's a good response, but it is still preliminary: it has to do with your intellectual curiosity about a bounded area of human knowledge. Now, if you respond, "I am trying to understand how to go about learning the secret of living fully," then you are raising "a religious or ultimate question": "A religious answer relates to the most profound meaning of one's existence."[61]

As this example suggests, ultimate concern can take a number of different forms. For example, it can be sacramental (worship-oriented), mystical, ethical, or even humanistic. Throughout history, in many different cultural contexts, it has been the product of different *revelations*, moments in which questions about the "profound meaning of one's existence" received an answer. As long as it is *ultimate* in the sense described above, however, a concern can be called religious.

This is not to say that Tillich simply excluded the vast world of preliminaries from his theory. In fact, he based much of his theology on a "method of correlation" which identifies the instances where the preliminary concern becomes "a medium, a vehicle, pointing beyond itself," i.e., towards the ultimate concern.[62] As you might imagine, this means that symbols are once again a focus. Tillich reminds us that the most basic function of symbols is to "point beyond themselves to something else," but they are distinct from everyday signs (like a stop light) because 1) they participate in the reality they represent (e.g., a president represents his nation but is also part of it), and 2) they reveal "levels of reality which otherwise are closed for us,"[63] so there's no way to know what it means for something to be profoundly beautiful without the symbols (in poetry, music, or paintings, for example) that take us there. Of course, words always point to something besides themselves, and ultimate concern always finds a name for itself: "God," for example, and all the characteristics commonly attributed to divine beings (power, love, justice, etc.). But symbols also take more concrete form: Tillich was fascinated by the way both myth and the arts (painting, poetry, music, sculpture, etc.) can point to and participate in "the depth dimension of reality itself, the dimension of reality which is the ground of every other dimension and every other depth ... the ultimate power of being."[64]

For Tillich (and for figures like Jung and Eliade as well) existentialism had characterized the plight of modern people: we find ourselves alienated from our own experience, wandering in a meaningless world, hungry for the *really real* truth of our existence that has been lost. Jung and Eliade presented generalized notions of that *really real* that sometimes had a theological ring to them. But Tillich was a Christian theologian, and so his answer to the existentialist challenge that faced all modern people was Christian. This leads us up to more tough questions, questions that come with playing along the border of the Second Order of Meaning (theology) and the Third Order of Meaning (the academic study of religion). Does Tillich's Christian commitment disqualify his theories for our use? Or did Tillich reach out far enough from his position on the inside to validate his theory for use in an academic setting? Once again, these are important questions to consider, but you should focus on the theoretical idea that can be derived from Tillich's approach: attempting to discern the ultimate concern for any religious individual, community, or tradition is a worthwhile experiment.

Tillich

The quote: "The concept of religion which makes ... a large extension of the meaning of the term possible is the following. Religion is the state of being grasped by an ultimate concern, a concern which qualifies all other concerns as preliminary and which itself contains the answer to the question of the meaning of our life ... The predominant religious name for the content of such concern is God—a god or gods. In nontheistic religions divine qualities are ascribed to a sacred object or an all-pervading power or a highest principle such as the Brahma or the One. In secular quasi-religions the ultimate concern is directed towards objects like nation, science, a particular form or stage of society, or a highest ideal of humanity, which are then considered divine."[65]

What to look for:

- The ultimate concern within a given religious tradition, or according to an individual practitioner.

- The way in which ultimate concern is symbolized in words, myths, and art.
- The expression and acting out of ultimate concern in seemingly non-religious ways.
- Whether religion responds effectively to existential dilemmas: why are we here, and how should we confront our finitude (death)?

W.C. Smith

The final figure treated in this chapter brings us back to one of the classic principles in the study of religion, articulated all the way back in Chapter 1: "He who knows one knows none." In his most famous work, *The Meaning and End of Religion*, theologian *Wilfred Cantwell Smith* (1916–2000) agreed and wrote, "One has not understood religion if one's interpretation is applicable to only one of its forms." But then he added, "neither has one understood religion if one's interpretation does justice only to some abstraction of religiousness in general but not to the fact that for most men of faith, loyalty and concern are not for any such abstraction but quite specifically and perhaps even exclusively for their own unique tradition—or even for one section within that."[66] With his emphasis on individual faith over intellectual abstractions, Smith's work raises a variety of crucial questions for the contemporary study of religion—not the least of which is whether an "academic" examination of it is desirable in the first place.

In *The Meaning and End of Religion*, abstractions consistently draw Smith's critical attention. As we saw in Chapter 2, he objects to the general term "religion," for example, because it allows us to disengage from "out-reaching faith,"[67] which is what religion is actually about. In addition, Smith notes that a general concept of "religion" or "religions" is unique to the West. While other traditions name themselves, they do so in terms that are particular and unique; they generally do not attempt to extend the terms they devise for themselves to other traditions, like the West has done with "religion." In keeping with its tendency to transform religion into a "thing," Western scholarship has generally failed to use native terms for other traditions and has instead made up its own labels for "religions," labels like Buddhism, Hinduism, Judaism, Taoism, Confucianism, etc.

As Smith notes, "Hinduism" is a particularly vivid example. This term was invented by the British as a catch-all to contend with an incredibly diverse range of doctrines and practices they found in India. Using the label "Hinduism" implies that all of these practices are somehow part of the same religious "system," but in actuality, "the mass of religious phenomena that we shelter under the umbrella of that term . . . is not a unity and does not aspire to be."[68] So in the case of Hinduism, the concept imposes a unity where it does not exist. But in the Chinese example, outsider concepts clearly divide. In China, an individual may engage in some practices that could be called "Confucian," others that would be considered "Taoist," and still others that are "Buddhist"—all within the space of an hour (or less). Given this way of dividing up the world, it is difficult to "imagine how a person can 'belong to three different religions' . . . at the same time". But here is the key point: "The perplexity arises not from something confused and bizarre about China so much as from the conceptualization of religious systems."[69] It's the categories that cause the confusion, not what's happening on the ground.

Smith provides a provocative basis for evaluating the terms and concepts we use in sorting out religious phenomena. But what is his positive program in presenting these critiques? What theory, or counter-theory of religion does he offer? When it comes to observing religion from the outside, Smith is concerned that abstractions distract us from the real heart of religion: the personal element of faith as a relationship with a higher power. If religion is just an abstract system, then it is possible (and acceptable) for an outside observer to limit their inquiry to its external trappings while simultaneously over-looking development, change, and diversity within the "cumulative tradition" associated with any given faith. If we *really* want to understand religion, then we must understand the "system" as an expression of a core experience, which is individual, deeply personal, and *not* dictated by outside categories. In short, for the academic observer, "[t]o know 'a religion' is not yet to know the religious life of him whom one observes."[70] We must instead aim "to discover and make known the personal faith of men that [religious] traditions have served."[71]

Smith's recommendations may or may not be persuasive in the academic study of religion, particularly because he often had a *religious* purpose in making them. On the one hand, as we saw in the Chinese example above, objectifying religion tends to produce and solidify differences between religious traditions, leading to tension and con-flict. Smith hoped that an analysis of comparative religions would lead to an appreciation of a common faith that is shared among all trad-itions. At the same time, Smith worried that the objectification of religion leads to "malaise," meaning that conceiving religion as a general system and thinking about one's religion as an "ism" com-partmentalizes religion as just one part of life, rather than taking it to be an all-encompassing concern. In other words, conceptualizing religion detracts from faith. Nevertheless, the lesson for the academic study of religion is clear: we must beware of our own abstractions because they can lead us to distortion and misunderstanding.

W.C. Smith

The quote: "What is profoundly important in the religious life of any people ... is that, whatever else it may be, religious life is a kind of *life*. Participants know this, consciously or unconsciously. Observers have to learn it. In learning it, they find that they must leave behind the distraction of congealed concepts postulating entities different from the living persons before them, or even theoretically independent of them ... The observer's concept of religion is by definition constituted of what can be observed. Yet the whole pith and substance of religious life lies in its relation to what cannot be observed."[72]

What to look for:

- Heartfelt expressions of individual faith and piety.
- The power of individual spirituality to promote change and development in a religious tradition.
- The power of individual faith to generate the most important expressions of a religious tradition.
- Native terms used to characterize, name, and describe a religious tradition.
- Places where general categories or labels fail to capture the complexity and particularity of religious phenomena.

Conclusion: Back to Plato's cave

So where does religion lie, inside Plato's cave or outside? In this chapter you have read about some strikingly different responses, and we can place them on a continuum. At one end we find theorists like Feuerbach, Marx, and Freud, who interpreted religious phenomena as projections, as the illusory shadows on the wall that keep people distracted from what's really true. On the other side we have figures like Tillich and Smith, who, while different from each other, generally agreed that the essence of religion was on the outside: maybe some of its elements were down in the darkness, but its essence was the light, the truth, and the way outside. Somewhere between are figures like Jung and Eliade: religions carry within them some essential, unique, universal truth, but like Plato himself, they suggested that it can only be revealed through theoretical insight and careful method.

Once again, for our purposes, the jury is still out on who is right in this debate. But as a beginner in the field, you should think carefully about how all of the classic theories in the field can make fundamental contributions to your ability to interpret religion. Note how all of the figures in the last two chapters offer compelling and distinctive options for defining, explaining, describing, and making predictions, some emphasizing one or more of these functions over the others, some balancing them evenly. In each case we find limitations, but in measuring these problems and testing these theoretical ideas, you join the broader effort to understand this strange, familiar thing that is religion.

Notes

[1] Karl Marx and Frederick Engels, *The German Ideology: Part One*, ed. C.J. Arthur (New York: International Publishers, 1986), 37.

[2] *Ibid.*, 42.

[3] *Ibid.*, 123.

[4] Karl Marx, "Contribution to the Critique of Hegel's *Philosophy of Right*: Introduction," in *The Marx-Engels Reader*, 2nd ed., ed. Robert C. Tucker (New York and London: W.W. Norton & Company, 1978), 53–4.

[5] *Ibid.*, 54.

[6] Marx and Engels, *The German Ideology: Part One*, 64.

[7] Marx, "Contribution to the Critique of Hegel's *Philosophy of Right*," 53–4.

[8] See Sigmund Freud, *The Future of an Illusion*, trans. James Strachey (New York and London: W.W. Norton & Company, 1961), 44.

[9] *Ibid.*, 10, 13.

[10] *Ibid.*, 15–16.

[11] *Ibid.*, 37.

[12] *Ibid.*, 24.

[13] *Ibid.*, 49.

[14] *Ibid.*, 43.

[15] C.G. Jung, *Psychology and Religion* (New Haven and London: Yale University Press, 1938), 3.

[16] Robert A. Segal, ed., *Encountering Jung: Jung on Mythology* (Princeton: Princeton University Press, 1998), 56.

[17] *Ibid.*, 63.

[18] C.G. Jung, *Answer to Job*, 2nd ed., trans. R.F.C. Hill (Princeton: Princeton University Press, 1973), xii.

[19] *Ibid.*, 63–4.

[20] *Ibid.*, 57–9.

[21] Jung, *Psychology and Religion*, 7.

[22] Segal, ed., *Jung on Mythology*, 83.

[23] *Ibid.*, 95.

[24] *Ibid.*, 41.

[25] *Ibid.*, 126.

[26] Jung, *Psychology and Religion*, 5.

[27] Mircea Eliade, *The Sacred and the Profane: The Nature of Religion*, trans. Willard R. Trask (San Diego and New York: Harcourt Brace Jovanovich, 1959), 10.

[28] *Ibid.*, 11.

[29] *Ibid.*, 64.

[30] *Ibid.*, 95.

[31] *Ibid.*, 100.

[32] *Ibid.*, 20.

[33] *Ibid.*, 21.

[34] *Ibid.*, 169.

[35] *Ibid.*, 68.

[36] *Ibid.*, 70.

[37] *Ibid.*, 14.

[38] Walter Capps, *Religious Studies: The Making of a Discipline* (Minneapolis, MN; Fortress Press, 1995), 145.

[39] Eliade, *The Sacred and the Profane*, 202.

[40] Ninian Smart, *Dimensions of the Sacred: An Anatomy of the World's Beliefs* (Berkeley and Los Angeles: University of California Press, 1996), 2.

[41] Ninian Smart, *Religions of Asia* (Englewood Cliffs, N.J.: Prentice Hall, 1993), 32.

[42] Smart, *Dimensions of the Sacred*, 2.

[43] Smart, *Religions of Asia*, 11, 17.

[44] Smart, *Dimensions of the Sacred*, 9.

[45] *Ibid.*, 10.

[46] *Ibid.*

[47] *Ibid.*, 132–3.

[48] *Ibid.*, 165.

[49] *Ibid.*

[50] *Ibid.*, 7.

[51] *Ibid.*, 4–5.

[52] Ninian Smart, *Beyond Ideology: Religion and the Future of Western Civilization* (San Francisco: Harper & Row, 1981), 47.

[53] Ninian Smart, *Concept and Empathy: Essay in the Study of Religion*, ed. Donald Wiebe (New York: New York University Press, 1986), 74–5.

[54] See Paul Tillich, *Systematic Theology: Volume 1* (Chicago: University of Chicago Press, 1951), 3–4.

[55] Paul Tillich, *Theology of Culture*, ed. Robert C. Kimball (New York: Oxford University Press, 1959), 9.

[56] Tillich, *Systematic Theology: Volume 1*, 12.

[57] Paul Tillich, *Dynamics of Faith* (New York: Harper & Row, 1957), 30–40.

[58] Tillich, *Systematic Theology: Volume 1*, 11–12.

[59] *Ibid.*, 14.

[60] The following example is adapted from Frederick J. Streng, *Understanding Religious Life*, 3rd ed. (Belmont, CA: Wadsworth Publishing Company, 1984), 7.

[61] *Ibid.*

[62] Tillich, *Systematic Theology: Volume 1*, 13.

[63] Tillich, *Dynamics of Faith*, 41–3.

[64] Tillich, *Theology of Culture*, 59.

[65] Paul Tillich, *Christianity and the Encounter of the World Religions* (New York and London: Columbia University Press, 1963), 4–5.

[66] Wilfred Cantwell Smith, *The Meaning and End of Religion* (Minneapolis, MN: Fortress Press, 1991), 3.

[67] *Ibid.*, 13.

[68] *Ibid.*, 66.

[69] *Ibid.*, 67–8.

[70] *Ibid.*, 135.

[71] *Ibid.*, 188–9.

[72] *Ibid.*, 136.

5 Conclusion: Where to go from here

The main premise of this book has been that religious worlds are constantly rushing up to us, calling out for interpretation. We must inform ourselves about the facts of these worlds, but we also need to know *how* to understand them, and that comes from careful consideration of theory and method.

Where to go from here? The most obvious answer: to the *content*, the rich material that we encounter; the texts, the rituals, the beliefs, the experiences, the testimonies, the symbols, the art, the material culture, the interaction with historical circumstance and the broader society—in short, to the "real stuff" of studying religion. This is where all the theoretical ideas you have learned about, the frames of reference that this book has provided, get put to the test. What "takes" or "angles" are going to work best? In what ways do the theories assist you in defining, describing, explaining, and making predictions about material you encounter? When will you be able to say that the bridge of understanding between academic outsider and the religious interior has been made?

Before you move on from these pages and start to tackle the "real stuff," however, be aware that the theories described in the previous chapters, while foundational and formative, hardly exhaust the array of approaches that populate the field today. New theoretical vistas open up in the academic study of religion all the time, as it responds to current events, cultural trends, and developments in other academic disciplines.

The conclusion to a book like this one has to emphasize these perspectives: while it has a fascinating history, the academic study of religion is a new, forward-looking field, and in this chapter, you are invited to look forward with it. Below you will find a survey of current, pressing issues in the field, the kinds of things scholars are working on today. In each case, these descriptions are brief and open-ended; they call upon you the student to take the next step by asking the right questions.[1] Grounded in the field's theoretical past, and now looking towards its horizons, you'll be on firm footing as you move forward.

Issues in the Study of Religion . . . Itself. As this book has often shown, the nature of the field itself has never been a simple or settled matter, and debates and controversies continue. Chapter 2, for example, included a discussion of the theology/religious studies divide; this issue continues to absorb scholars' attention.[2] In addition, we have often examined the question of bias in the modern study of religion. In reflecting on the legacy of the classic theorists, contemporary observers have engaged in ever more sophisticated modes of critical self-reflection.

For example, thinking back to our theorists in Chapters 3 and 4, you might have noticed that a lot of them were Germans, and all of them were European or American. According to some critics, the intellectual assumptions of these thinkers (borrowed from the European Enlightenment or Romanticism) produced an inevitable bias: the religion scholar stands above the material he or she is investigating. This superior position of the Western intellectual corresponds with an economic and political arrangement that dominated throughout much of the modern period: *colonialism*, the European and American occupation of the so-called "Third World" for political and economic gains.

Has this connection between scholarship and colonialism affected the way that other religions are viewed? Perhaps so. Some contemporary critics argue, for example, that Westerners often think about Asian religions as mystical, dreamy, irrational, and passive because that characterization highlights the supposed identity of the Westerner as clear-headed, rational, and active—and most importantly, fit to rule over the lands of "the East." This attitude has been called *Orientalism*, and those who have examined it claim that the subjugation of other lands has distorted the academic study of religion.[3]

Another thing about our classic theorists: almost all of them came from a Christian background (Freud and Marx are major exceptions), and many were Protestant. Despite its persistent attempt to clear away prejudices, some would argue that the discipline still contains religious biases that are part of the backdrop of modern Western culture. Critics have proposed, for example, that it continues to emphasize texts, doctrines (belief in God, in particular), and private experiences, which are crucial elements of the Protestant worldview. This results in a narrow, biased framework for interpreting other traditions.

Pushing even further, many contemporary scholars also pick up on an *essentialist* bias in the modern study of religion. What does this mean? Recall how often the theorists in previous chapters tried to nail down an absolute essence, that which is *sui generis* ("of its own kind") in religion the world over. While this quest is one of the things that makes these theories compelling, it can also lead to narrow or simplified accounts. As we have seen, identifying religion as the worship of God/gods is an *essentialism* that has misleading results, but so may be identifying it exclusively with "the holy," "the sacred," the "liminal," economics, psycho-sexual development, the "collective unconscious," or "ultimate concern." Throughout, this book has attempted to prize the distinctiveness of these interpretations, while also recommending a *pluralist* attitude that can serve as an antidote to essentialism.[4]

Finally, in his own way, Wilfred Cantwell Smith was on the cutting edge. While approaching the issue from a different perspective, a number of contemporary theorists have renewed the critique of the abstractions that are commonplace in our characterization of "world religions."[5] We need handles like "Christianity," "Judaism," "Hinduism," "Buddhism," "Taoism," etc. to serve as general placeholders, but some argue that we tend to get stuck on these labels, leading to a quest for the single essence of a tradition, rather than a confrontation with its diversity, complexity, and richness. Let's at least be sure, they would propose, that we talk about "Christianities," "Judaisms," "Hinduisms," and so on, while also recognizing that religion takes place in particular historical, social and economic contexts.

As you can see, the field thrives on continuing discussions about *how* religion should be studied, and now is a time when that basic methodological principle, *self-consciousness*, is of particular concern. As a result, keep some essential questions in mind as you encounter the "real stuff". *How much does the European/American identity of religious studies affect the way it approaches traditions from the rest of the world? Does the academic study of religion still bear the imprint of a particular religious perspective? What is missed by searching for a singular, universal essence to religion? How can we use general labels in the study of religion in a way that avoids their potential pitfalls?*

Religion and Gender. You might have noticed something else about the classic theorists surveyed in Chapter 3 and 4: they were all men. That doesn't necessarily mean anything in itself. But in this case, some critics have argued that it symbolizes a significant bias within the modern study of religion: women's experience has not been on the agenda. Feeling the impact of feminism, recent scholars have been working to identify and remedy this problem.[6]

In a broad sense, *gender* is a vital issue in the study of any culture. Religion in particular plays a vital role in the *construction* of gender, the way it is understood and imagined, both at the level of *social conduct* (the roles assigned to the two sexes, along with the rules that dictate their behavior) and the *symbolic imagination* (the way that the masculine and feminine principles are imagined and portrayed, in the figures of gods and goddesses, for example). The problem with the study of religion, at least up until recent decades, was that it seemed to share *patriarchal* assumptions with Western culture at large: the experience and perspective of men were taken to be normative for any given tradition or community.

Recent scholarship has criticized these assumptions, leading to a more even-handed, thoroughgoing analysis. "Gendering" religious studies involves listening for the distinctions between the way men and women experience and conceive their religious identity. It also leads to analysis of the construction of gender within religious systems, with particular sensitivity to the distribution of *power*. Who is in charge of what sphere of life, and even when men are thought to be dominant, do women find alternative ways of gaining authority? In addition, thinking about gender and religion involves *comparison*: gender is constructed variously in different traditions, so it is important to compare traditions in which women and the feminine principle are esteemed, for instance, with those that uphold patriarchal assumptions.

Overall, "changing the subject" in religious studies[7] to take account of gender is one vital way to ensure that the *fullness* of the phenomenon is before us, and not just part of it. As a result, we need to ask: *how might focusing on women alter our theoretical approach to the study of religion? What role do women play in any given religious community, is their experience of religion distinctive and how have religious traditions contributed to the way gender is understood in the cultures to which they belong?*

Religion, Sexuality and the Body. "Changing the subject" to reflect gender and women's experience has often been accompanied by careful reflection on sex. As recent scholarship has shown, throughout history, religion has played a major role in constructing sexuality.[8] Again, we can think about this issue at the level of *social conduct* and as an aspect of the *symbolic imagination*. Religions often dictate the sexual conduct of their adherents, regulating what behaviors are encouraged, allowed, and prohibited. Sex can also be a vital aspect of religious imagery and theology. The creation of the universe, for example, can be conceived as the product of a sexual act. From an overarching Freudian perspective, of course, much of the religious life is the product of a sexual, *libidinal* drive that is repressed and re-channeled into both beliefs and practices.

We should also note that a more open environment for examining both gender and sexuality has opened the door to gay and lesbian perspectives. As was the case with "changing the subject" of religious studies to address women's experience, "que(e)rying religion" has aimed to recapture the experience of gays and lesbians within religious contexts.[9] Placing this concern on the agenda adds yet another intriguing layer to theorizing about religion's impact on social conduct, the symbolic imagination and the complex identity of individual adherents.

Examination of sex and sexuality can be situated within an even broader concern: the relationship between the body and religion.[10] It's easy to get fixated on the intellectual or emotional aspects of religious life—the beliefs, doctrines, and feelings that accompany it—but that can distract from the *embodied* aspect of religious life. The only way to *be* in the world is to be in a body, and religious traditions always have something to say about it: how to manage it, how to shape it, how to adorn it, how to move with it. Rituals, of course, are embodied practices, so some recent scholars direct our attention not only to what a practice *means* but also how it is *performed*, how it is experienced as a bodily event. In addition, religious traditions present many fascinating theories about the body and its true nature, but they also employ the imagery of the body to clarify and explain our position in the world—conceiving it, for example, as the body of God/a god, or marking off sacred spaces as locations where the divine body made contact with it.

While our classic theorists often considered sex, sexuality and the body in their work, recent scholars have pushed this analysis to new levels of sophistication—and you can join them. Ask yourself: *what does any given religious tradition or community have to say about sex? How is it regulated or imagined, and where does it break through in unexpected ways? How is the body conceived? Is being embodied a distinctive way of experiencing the world religiously?*

Religion, Race, and Ethnicity. Another limitation within the study of religion up until recent times is its failure to take account of the *diversity* of racial and ethnic perspectives. Many contemporary theorists have argued that a white, Eurocentric perspective has consistently denied the rich tapestry of human identity and experience. Religious studies has actually taken a leading role in challenging this narrow perspective because its subject matter is inherently global in scope, and contemporary scholars continue to ensure that both race and ethnicity are on the field's agenda.

Like religion, race and ethnicity are complicated concepts, but recent scholarship has tried to sort things out by working in two different directions. First, we can start with racial and ethnic communities and examine the ways in which they experience, re-imag-ine, and make religious traditions part of their identity. For example, how has the African American experience affected the way this community understands Christianity? What are the differences between Irish Catholicism and, say, Catholicism in Latin America, between Methodism in the United States and in Korea, between evangelical Protestantism in America and in Africa, and so on? How has Buddhism been constructed in diverse national contexts, like Tibet or Japan? Questions like these point out religion's power to supplement a group's sense of identity, solidarity, and distinctiveness. They also indicate yet another strand of diversification within traditions that are sometimes thought to be monolithic.

Taking another approach, scholars have also shown that a culture's concepts of race and ethnicity are a product of religious sensibilities.[11] So, for example, how has the interpretation of scriptures, like the Bible or the Hindu Vedas, contributed to the way that races and nations are understood in their cultural contexts? Has Christianity contributed to what it means to be "black" or "white" in Europe or America? What about the complex example of Judaism, within which religion and ethnicity are so tightly intertwined? Does being a Hindu call for belonging to a certain national identity? While these kinds of questions emphasize differences, we should also note that religions often attempt to transcend these boundaries, opening a path to salvation or liberation to anyone, regardless of culture, nation, or skin color.

As is the case with gender and sexuality, placing an emphasis on the intersections between race, ethnicity, and religion gets us thinking about *identity*, or the *multiple identities* that constitute a person's worldview. If we are to understand our fellow human beings, our study of their religion must take account of these multiple dimensions. *How does an individual or community's racial and/or ethnic identity affect its religious sensibilities? How has religion contributed to our notions of race and ethnicity?*

Religion and its Innovations. It could be said that religions are nothing without change. It is part of the nature of a *tradition* to preserve continuity, but tradition also absorbs change and lets it unfold. At the same time, we also discover many examples of radical shifts, striking reinventions, and the emergence of new forms that seem to come out of the blue. The contemporary study of religion is particularly sensitive to these shifts, in keeping with a world that is in constant flux.

Religious traditions have always had a habit of splitting as a result of doctrinal disagreements, political disputes, or reform movements instigated by prophetic or contemplative leaders. Recent decades have seen a trend towards innovations of a particular kind: small, splinter groups breaking off from mainstream religion and society, often led to an isolated, communal lifestyle by a charismatic figure. Groups like these are often known as "cults" in the popular media, but scholars prefer to call them "New Religious Movements," or NRMs for short.[12]

In Chapters 1 and 2, we already considered the unique challenges that these groups pose. For one thing, they don't fit within our usual understanding of the big "world religions"; they are neither officially sanctioned nor particularly representative. At times they are also *syncretistic*: they borrow from a number of different traditions and piece together a unique new worldview. Most challenging, perhaps, is the intense devotion that the followers of these relatively new movements display, a commitment that has, on occasion, led to confrontation, murder and martyrdom. In analyzing groups like Jim Jones's People's Temple, the Branch Davidians at Waco, Aum Shinrikyo (Japan), ISKCON (the International Society for Krishna Consciousness, i.e., the Hare Krishnas), the Nation of Islam, Falun Gong (China), or even Scientology, we need to take full advantage of our theoretical tools. And at the same time, we might recall that the "New Religious Movement" of today has the potential to become the "religion" of tomorrow!

On a broader front, many scholars have also been exploring the implications of *globalization*, the ongoing worldwide trend towards the breakdown of political, cultural, and economic boundaries. This "new world order" has resulted in unprecedented communication and mobility—and a religious situation that is often an intricate mixture of "crossing and dwelling."[13]

Immigrants have always had a distinctive experience as they make their way in a foreign land: do they assimilate, stay withdrawn in their own enclaves, or find an accommodation somewhere in between? Religion has often been a major factor in these deliberations, especially when the religious sensibilities of the new land are at odds with those of the immigrant. Residing in a place where a tradition other than one's own dominates can present a difficulty, but a *religiously plural* environment can be just as tricky.

In the new, globalized situation, something else has been added to the mix: many immigrants are committed to making a life in their adopted nation, but technology and mobility allow them to maintain close connections with the homeland. This experience can add complications. After all, where is *home*? In the country of one's origin, where most of the family still resides, where one's culture is ubiquitous, where the most significant religious centers are located? Or is home in the new land, where one lives and works, perhaps within a *diaspora* community, which maintains material and symbolic ties to the native culture and religion? Things get even more interesting when the diasporic individual has a largely secular lifestyle in one locale (or one that fits with its foreign culture), and then reverts to her own traditions in the homeland. Contemporary theorists have shown that this condition is now common, and they have called it *hybridity*: belonging to two or more worldviews at once.[14]

Religion is often caught in the interplay of the multiple identities that the citizens of a globalized world often possess. But some would argue that these complexities, experienced by individuals on the ground, are merely the signs of much larger trends. In particular, some observers emphasize the homogenizing effects of globalization: the tendency for old national boundaries to break down, for cultural differences to be diluted. Religion is a difference that many of our fellow human beings hold onto for dear life, and yet globalization may be urging it towards universality and standardization, as more people make accommodations with a wider world.

When it comes to religion and its innovations, we must also recall the huge, vague movement that puts many of our theoretical models to the test: *spirituality*, or a "New Age" outlook. Particularly in America, but surely in many other places as well, it is common to find people who say that they are "spiritual," not "religious," meaning that for them religion should be a matter of individual choice, feeling, and conscience, not a socially dictated phenomenon. New Age, spiritual seekers assemble their own beliefs and practices, picking and choosing from many traditions based on their needs, and constructing a therapeutic worldview that is subject to constant adjustment. Given the prevalence of this perspective, students of religion have to wonder whether following this lead is a good idea. Perhaps the emphasis on personal choice and individual experience is rapidly becoming the core of contemporary religion. At the same time, this viewpoint remains quite unfamiliar for most religious people across the globe, mostly because it privatizes and compartmentalizes the "spiritual" life far too much.

Change has always been a basic characteristic of religions, and in our dynamic age, we have to be all the more sensitive to it by posing the right questions. *How should we study New Religious Movements? What theoretical tools will best help us to understand these new developments on the religious landscape? How have immigration and globalization affected the development of religions and concepts of religious identity? And what about being "spiritual, not religious"? Is this an adequate distinction? Is it a good starting point for the interpretation of religion?*

Religion and its Theologies: Fundamentalist and Liberal.
While NRMs, syncretistic worldviews, and spiritual seekers tend to
chart out innovative, non-traditional territory for their religious
expression, there are other forces at work within the world's major
religions that are striving to bring them back to their foundations.
These movements are often called *fundamentalist*. This is a much
debated term among scholars, but in general, fundamentalists react to
the perceived encroachments of modern, secular life by urging a
return to the absolute "fundamentals" of the tradition: say, for
Christians, a literalist interpretation of the Bible and direct encounter
with the saving power of Jesus Christ; for Jews, strict adherence to
Torah and religious law; for Hindus, the Vedas and Aryan identity; or
in Islam, the Qur'an and the model of the original Muslim community of the prophet. While core beliefs are vital in these movements, however, they are just as much about finding a place in a
complex world. Strictly (literally) speaking, for example, there is
nothing in the Bible about the modern abortion procedure, and yet
Christian fundamentalists are unanimous in their rejection of the
practice. The point is that *fundamentalism* is a modern phenomenon,
because it is a reaction to the elements of modern, pluralistic, generally secular societies.[15]

In contrast, other movements have attempted to move in the
opposite direction, towards a *better* accommodation with the secular
world and other religious traditions, while often promoting pro-
gressive social change. Unitarian Universalism is one of the best
examples of a religious group that has liberal tolerance embedded in
its "fundamental" beliefs. Reform Judaism is another movement that
prides itself on accommodation with reason and liberal principles.
Strands of modern Theravada Buddhism have also claimed a connection between the Buddha's teachings, modern science, and secular
common sense. Christianity has even matched up with Marxism, in
the Liberation Theology movements that arose in Latin America
during the 1970s.

Of course, from an insider's perspective, liberal theological
movements can be cause for concern: Where does the accommodation stop? When does a tradition have to assert its own difference in
the face of a non-religious society, and in relation to other religious
worldviews? *Answering* such questions is the responsibility of insiders;
as students of religion, our job is to describe and explain these
dynamics. In general, the same goes for *fundamentalism*, which first
and foremost raises its protest against members of its own tradition.
However, interpreting it is obviously a pressing concern in the
academic study of religion: in a few cases, as we know too well,

fundamentalists are bent on eliminating the religious and cultural competition; it is the job of the religion scholar to try to understand why.

In all major religions there is a wide spectrum between fundamentalism and liberalism. We should stay alert to that diversity—and to the position of insiders within these debates, insiders who may be the ones informing the student of religion about the interior of their tradition. *How do religious traditions react to the challenge of religious pluralism and secular life? When should we consider a movement "fundamentalist"? Why does fundamentalism arise? What are instances of religions attempting to reach out to the secular world and other traditions, and what have been the results?*

Religion and Violence (and Peace). When we began to reflect on the question "Why study religion today?" in the opening to this book, the most obvious answer was religious violence. There is no denying the fact that religion has often become linked to violent struggle and conflict in the popular imagination. Of course, Islamic terrorism is the example that leaps to most people's minds, but current scholarship tempers this fixation by reminding us that no tradition is innocent: not Christianity, with its injunction to "turn the other cheek," not Judaism, with its emphasis on ethics and law, not Hinduism, with its tolerant conception of diversity in unity, not even Buddhism, with its emphasis on *ahimsa*, or "not harming." How is it that religions turn violent?[16]

Obviously there is no universal, clear-cut answer to this question. Some authors have argued that religion—or particular religions—are inherently violent in nature.[17] For one thing, religion requires the individual to subordinate himself to a higher authority, whether institutional or divine. This constitutes a violent sacrifice of the self, of the individual's mind and personality. The energy that is suppressed in this quintessentially religious act comes out in intense feelings of insider belonging, what Durkheim called "collective effervescence." Given this intense insider devotion, it makes sense that those on the outside are seen as profane or impure—they become the infidels, the heretics, the *scapegoats* that can been sacrificed on the altar of religious solidarity. In other words, something like a mob mentality lurks just beneath the surface in religious contexts, and while violent urges are most often kept in check, sometimes, if the circumstances are right, they come to the surface and erupt. In sum, religion promotes both irrationality and division—a dangerous combination.

Other perspectives are more measured. Elements within a religious tradition may enable violence, and as students, we must not shy away from the more jarring episodes that are front and center in some traditions. But careful scholarship reminds us that it takes a combination of forces (social, economic, political etc.) to push communities over the edge. To this extent, fixating on religion is an interpretive mistake because it often serves as more of an emblem or rallying cry than a singular *cause* for violence and war. While it is indeed surprising that in many cases, religions cannot stand up to these forces, especially for all their talk about peace, careful analysis also reveals the circumstances under which it can be molded by other forces to justify horrifying acts.

Despite their tremendous potential for enabling conflict, many would argue that religions also contain resources for peaceful solutions and social progress. While it is naïve to say that all religions are essentially peaceful at their heart (as we have seen, such generalizations only work to a certain extent, if at all), they have fostered many great social movements for peace. There is an indelible image from the beginning of the Vietnam War, for example, that depicts a Buddhist monk calmly immolating himself—setting himself on fire—in a stunning protest against the violence. Religious figures have devoted their lives to justice, dialogue, and reconciliation, often with great success, figures like Mahatma Gandhi in India, Martin Luther King in the United States, and Archbishop Desmond Tutu in South Africa. With so much attention to bloodshed, it is important to keep this counter-balance in mind: the vast majority of religious people live a relatively non-offensive existence, and their traditions often contribute to keeping the peace.

With this balance in mind, you will be in a good position to start working on questions that are very much on the cutting edge in the field. *Why does religious violence happen? Is religion inherently violent? Do certain religious traditions (or particular interpretations of them) have more potential for giving rise to violence? What forces are at work in specific instances of "religious violence"? How have religions contributed to the cause of peace, justice and reconciliation?*

Religion and Science. Religion and science have often been conceived as enemies: religion is based on faith, whereas science relies on reason. While this dichotomy is simplistic, the rapid emergence of science and technology in the modern age has challenged religious worldviews, sometimes shaking them to the core. And at the same time, the persistence of religion has often perplexed scientifically minded observers, and in our day and age, a number of them have renewed the calls for its demise.[18] The academic study of religion prizes a more moderate perspective. There is little doubt that the history of the interaction between religion and science is much more complicated than it is usually taken to be.[19] In addition, contemporary science adds compelling new insights to our understanding of religious phenomena.

One very prominent example of the conflict between religion and science is the debate over creationism (or intelligent design) *versus* evolution. At the most basic level, this discussion is *cosmological*. For example, many religious traditions contain accounts of the beginnings of the universe that can be called into question by scientific analysis. The controversy is particularly vivid in contexts where the Bible is authoritative because it presents a single narrative of God's creation that can, if read literally, be placed in actual historical time (i.e., the world was created some 6,000 years ago). Science presents overwhelming evidence to the contrary, dating our world at 4 or 5 billion years old, and tracing the universe back to 10 billion years old. Of course, there is little room for compromise between these perspectives.

The controversy gets even more tangled when the focus turns to the *origins of life*. Religious thinkers have often employed the apparent design of the world, and particularly the design of biological entities within it, to support belief in the existence of a single intelligent designer, i.e., God. In a way, science comes to the aid of this argument. How could something as complex or nuanced as the human eye, for example, be a random shot in the dark? Didn't someone or something have to craft it, intentionally? Doesn't science continue to show us the ingenuity at work behind such features of the organic world? In the wake of the evolutionary theory proposed by *Charles Darwin* (1809–82), scientists have argued that, indeed, the eye came from a process of randomness and selection that extended over millions of years. There was no divine blueprint for organisms, only a long history of adaptations that were gradually selected out to make survival more likely. Again, scientific evidence in support of this theory is overwhelming, yet it flatly contradicts a central belief in so many religious traditions: human beings were made by and in the image of the divine.

This is not the right place to try to adjudicate these controversies, yet they provide the backdrop for cutting-edge approaches in the study of religion that employ evolutionary psychology, cognitive science, and neuroscience. Religion, some scholars have argued, was a *product* of human evolution: it served to protect us from otherwise overwhelming fears, while also promoting social cohesion that was vital to human survival. As part of this process, religious practices also lit up parts of the human brain in productive ways that can now be charted by new imaging technologies. Some researchers have actually mapped out what happens in the brain when a monk meditates or a disciple worships, and cognitive science is beginning to account for the religious beliefs that help adherents maintain an ordered, meaningful experience of the world—including the belief in God/gods.[20]

A related area of research pertains to the relationship between religion and medical science. There is a long history of religious healers who drew upon myth and ritual to get positive psychological and physiological results from their patients. Scholars have shown that these practices sometimes had a medical basis. But obviously modern science represents an entirely different worldview, and religious traditions often find themselves at odds with medical practices that violate their basic principles. The abortion, stem-cell and euthanasia debates are good examples, as is the case of Jehovah's Witnesses, who refuse to receive any blood transfusions. Genetic therapy is another challenging prospect, because for some it crosses into territory that should be off-limits: the design, manipulation, and perhaps even *creation* of human existence.

Even this quick survey should give you a sense of the huge territory that is being opened up in the area of science and religion. The scientific research is unfolding quickly, so quickly that it can be overwhelming. And yet it is incumbent on students of religion to stay on top of this developing field. *What is the historical relationship between religions and science? How have they influenced each other? How does evolution affect our approach to the study of religion? How do evolutionary psychology, cognitive science, and neuroscience affect our perspective on religion? Where have religious traditions and medicine intersected, and in what instances are they in conflict?*

Religion and the Environment. Another area of connection between science and religion is in the realm of ecology. For many, only the most basic operation of experimental science, *observation*, is necessary to see the effects of environmental degradation and climate change.

For the student of religion, one of the most interesting avenues of approach to any religious tradition is its concept of nature.[21] In the Judeo-Christian worldview, for example, scholars have explored the basic theological assumption that God created man in his image and gave him dominion over all of creation. This separation of both God and man from nature, one could argue, has been a premise for exploiting it. Some ecologically minded historians of religion also point out that the appearance of the "Father God," who is distant from and in some sense opposed to nature, suppressed a *matriarchal* tradition that privileged the feminine principle: "Mother Earth" or "Gaia." This ancient tradition was much more respectful of the earth because it was conceived to be divine, but this perspective has been suppressed in Western civilization for nearly three millennia. As a rejoinder to these critiques, some interpreters point out that the Bible also inserts an element of responsibility: God took great pride in his creation and made humankind its responsible steward, and especially in the modern, industrial West, we have dramatically failed in this duty.

Reaching beyond the biblical tradition, we find that situating religious belief and practice much closer to nature is a common phenomenon. How would we look at the environment differently if God/the gods were somehow *in it*, and not outside it? Indigenous traditions, including many Native American traditions, often uphold this belief: there's an old story about a tribesman in Africa who trips over a stone and then turns around and says, "Oh, sorry. Excuse me." Paganism is a new/old religious movement that also attempts to re-evaluate the human relationship to the natural world. In some of the major "world religions" too, we discover a commitment to the interconnectedness of all things, leading to a different perspective on nature. In Hinduism and Buddhism, for example, all life is thought to be part of the same cycle of birth and re-birth, leading to a basic commitment to *ahimsa*, or "refraining from harm" to all sentient beings. In addition, some forms of Taoism see nature as the quint-essential model for following the true Way (Tao) that operates behind all things; nature is the absolute authority, not scriptures, not humans, not gods. This is not to say that all practitioners of these traditions (and others like them) are "environmentally conscious," but explor-ing these worldviews gives us some perspective on an issue that is at the forefront of our cultural and political consciousness.

So, as a student of religion, when you encounter the "real stuff" of religion, keep nature in mind. This will not only give you better insight into the subject matter; it will also shed some light on one of the most pressing concerns of our generation. *How does a tradition conceive of nature in its myths, scriptures, and beliefs? What natural symbols are present? Is nature something to be protected, suppressed, or disregarded? How do religions relate to contemporary environmental consciousness?*

Religion and the Spectacle of the Arts and the Media. Once again recalling our classic theorists from Chapters 3 and 4, we had numerous opportunities to reflect on the symbolic, material, and aesthetic components of religious life. Durkheim, for example, ana-lyzed the power of sacred totems that represent group identity, and he found that tribe members adorn their lives with these symbolic representations and make them the center of ritual practices. Geertz's first assumption about religion was that it is "a system of symbols," which often take material form in the lives of practitioners, like a cross that hangs around a Christian's neck. Freud and Jung also devoted considerable attention to symbols because they refer to deep, often unspoken realities that stand behind religious consciousness. Finally, Paul Tillich's "method of correlation" led him to explore the link between symbols, art, and the foundation of religious faith, "ultimate concern."[22]

Scholars in the field have continued to follow these directions in analyzing the connection between the religious, the material, and the aesthetic. On the most basic level, the material dimension of religion (to use Ninian Smart's category) includes the objects associated with ritual practice and everyday life. These objects are innumerable: a postcard depicting the Hindu god Ganesh on a dashboard; the *mezuzah* on the doorframe marking a Jewish home; the rosary beads around the wrist of an Catholic or a Buddhist; the white *ihram* garment donned by Muslims undertaking the *hajj*; the book of scripture itself, the Bible, the Qur'an, the Torah scroll; the plastic, illuminated manger scene in an American front yard; and a chunk of marble with the Ten Commandments inscribed on it, (not) in city hall. We should also include sound in this material, aesthetic dimension: the bells and whistles of religion that announce or add to the intensity of ritual, along with the songs and chants practitioners perform. Many scholars find this dimension of religion the most interesting, because these objects are intimate treasures that carry a wealth of meaning for the individual worshiper and the community.

But at some point it is necessary to make a distinction between these intimate objects and "high religious art," which is clearly designed to make a spectacle: at times it is difficult to determine whether the art serves the religion or religion serves the art! Here we can include magnificent examples of religious painting, statuary, and textiles, and the monumental buildings that contain them. We might think of the great European cathedrals and their contents; the huge Tibetan tapestries depicting mandalas, complex ritual diagrams depicting holy people and cosmic regions; or massive statues, like the 60-foot tall depictions in stone of Jain saints in India. At the same time, the artistic dimension of religion takes other monumental shapes, in music, like Handel's *Messiah*, for example, or in literature, like Dante's *Divine Comedy*.

Modern artistic production has a life of its own, and yet, as many observers have shown, it continues to be attracted to religious content. In addition, contemporary forms of technology often mediate the religious spectacle, on both a grand and intimate scale. Religious themes permeate popular forms of entertainment, including music, film, sports, and television.[23] Practitioners have also turned to new media to get their message out and even to worship. Christian preachers have always made their presence known on American television, for example, and some of them even suggest that touching the screen makes a connection to the Holy Spirit. In another striking development, some Hindu websites present the image of a god and urge worshipers to take its *darshan* online, thus engaging in a form of reverence where the devotee sees the god—and the god looks back.[24]

Where these new forms of mediated religion will go is a wide-open question. At the very least, religious literacy is an absolute requirement for studying the history of art in almost any cultural context. At the same time, it prepares us for whatever new forms of the religious spectacle come our way. *How do ritual and everyday objects express the religious worldview to which they belong? What is the best way to read and interpret grander examples of religious art? What religious themes can be discerned in modern art? To what extent is living a religious life similar to living an artistic life? And how do new technologies and media affect religious experience?*

Religion and Dwelling ... Again. By way of conclusion, we return to our old friend William James, who had this to say about his passionate interest in this strange, familiar thing called religion:

> Religion, whatever it is, is a man's total reaction upon life, so why not say that any total reaction upon life is a religion? ... To get at [total reactions] you must go behind the foreground of existence and reach down to that curious sense of the whole residual cosmos as an everlasting presence ... This sense of the world's presence, appealing as it does to our peculiar individual temperament, makes us either strenuous or careless, devout or blasphemous, gloomy or exultant, about life at large; and our reaction ... is the completest of all our answers to the question, "What is the character of this universe in which we dwell?"[25]

We know by now how to put this view in perspective: James thought that the foundational element of religion, its Zero Order, was an unseen, underlying realm (here characterized as "the whole residual cosmos as an everlasting presence") that makes itself known through an individual, pre-rational encounter. You now have the tools to reflect on this view, to test its strengths and weaknesses, to determine the value of this "theoretical idea."

But also take note of the sentiments here that are indispensable for any student of religion. James urges you to "go behind the foreground of existence," to see what's behind religious phenomena. That is the primary goal of *theoretical literacy*: to interpret this subject matter in a methodologically self-conscious way; to employ definition, explanation, description, and prediction effectively; and thus to reach a better understanding. James also brings us back to the very beginning, to that idea from J.Z. Smith, who proposed that "What we study when we study religion is one mode of constructing worlds of meaning, worlds within which men find themselves and in which they choose to dwell." As you are beginning to discover, these worlds are endlessly fascinating, and in our day and age, they call out for your attention.

At the same time, the study of religion is its own dwelling place, something of a shelter in the midst of a swirl of strange, familiar possibilities. I do hope that in reading this book, you have begun to feel at home in it.

Notes

1   For an excellent, in-depth compendium of current issues in the study of religion, see *The Routledge Companion to the Study of Religion*, ed. John R. Hinnells (London and New York: Routledge, 2005).

2   See *Religious Studies, Theology, and the University: Conflicting Maps, Changing Terrain*, ed. Linell E. Cady and Delwin Brown (Albany: State University of New York Press, 2002); *Religious Studies and Theology: An Introduction*, ed. Helen K. Bond, Seth D. Kunin, and Francesca Aran Murphy (New York: New York University Press, 2003); and *Fields of Faith: Theology and Religious Studies for the Twenty-first Century*, ed. David F. Ford, Ben Quash, and Janet Martin Soskice (Cambridge: Cambridge University Press, 2005).

3   Consult Richard King *Orientalism and Religion: Postcolonial theory, India and 'The Mystic East'* (London and New York: Routledge, 1999).

4   A challenging collection that takes a postmodern, anti-essentialist approach to the study of religion: *Critical Terms for Religious Studies*, ed. Mark C. Taylor (Chicago and London: The University of Chicago Press, 1998).

5   See *The Invention of World Religions: Or, How European Universalism Was Preserved in the Language of Pluralism* (Chicago and London : The University of Chicago Press, 2005).

6   For an excellent starting point for research in this area, see *Religion and Gender*, ed. Ursula King (Oxford and Malden, MA: Blackwell Publishers, 1995). Also consult *Today's Woman in World Religions*, ed. Arvind Sharma (Albany: State University of New York Press, 1994) and *Feminism in the Study of Religion: A Reader*, ed. Darlene Juschka (London and New York: Continuum, 2001).

7   A reference to Mary McClintock Fulkerson, *Changing the Subject: Women's Discourses and Feminist Theology* (Minneapolis, MN: Fortress Press, 1994).

8   See *Sexuality and World's Religions*, ed. David W. Machachek and Melissa M. Wilcox (Santa Barbara, CA: ABC-Clio, 2003).

[9]   *Que(e)rying Religion: A Critical Anthology*, ed. Gary David Comstock and
      Susan E. Henking (London and New York: Continuum, 1997).

[10] The most notable collection on this topic remains *Religion and the Body*,
      ed. Sarah Coakley (Cambridge: Cambridge University Press, 1997).

[11] See *Religion and the Creation of Race and Ethnicity: An Introduction*, ed. Craig
      R. Prentiss (New York: New York University Press, 2003).

[12] For additional reading on this topic see *Cults and New Religious Movements:
      A Reader*, ed. Lorne L. Dawson (Oxford and Malden, MA: 2003); Lorne
      L. Dawson, *Comprehending Cults: The Sociology of New Religious Movements*,
      2nd ed. (New York: Oxford University Press, 2006); and *Cults, Religion,
      and Violence*, ed. David G. Bromley and J. Gordon Melton (Cambridge:
      Cambridge University Press, 2002).

[13] Thomas A. Tweed, *Crossing and Dwelling: A Theory of Religion* by (Cam-
      bridge: Harvard University Press, 2006) is particularly sensitive to mobil-
      ity, migrancy, and diaspora, which are characteristic of globalized religion.
      For a comprehensive treatment of these issues, also see *The Oxford
      Handbook of Global Religions*, ed. Mark Juergensmeyer (New York: Oxford
      University Press, 2006).

[14] For treatments of religion, diaspora, and the immigrant experience, see
      Gatherings in Diaspora: Religious Communities and the New Immigration, ed.
      R. Stephen Warner and Judith G. Wittner (Philadelphia: Temple Uni-
      versity Press, 1998) and Diana L. Eck, *A New Religious America: How a
      "Christian Country" Has Become the World's Most Religiously Diverse Nation*
      (New York: HarperCollins, 2001).

[15] See Karen Armstrong, *The Battle for God* (New York: Ballantine, 2000);
      Gabriel A. Almond, R. Scott Appleby and Emmanuel Silvan, *Strong
      Religion: The Rise of Fundamentalisms around the World* (Chicago and
      London: The University of Chicago Press, 2003) and *Accounting for Fun-
      damentalisms: The Dynamic Character of Movements* (Chicago and London:
      The University of Chicago Press, 2004).

[16] Two striking accounts of this issue can be found in Mark Juergensmeyer,
      Terror and the Mind of God: The Global Rise of Religious Violence, 3rd ed.
      (Berkeley: University of California Press, 2003); and Bruce Lincoln, *Holy
      Terrors: Thinking about Religion after September 11*, 2nd ed. (Chicago and
      London: The University of Chicago Press, 2006).

[17] A number of popular books supporting this perspective have appeared in
      the last few years, including Sam Harris, *The End of Faith: Religion, Terror,
      and the Future of Reason* (New York and London: W.W. Norton &
      Company, 2005) and Christopher Hitchens, *God Is Not Great: How
      Religion Poisons Everything* (New York: Hachette Book Group, 2007).

[18] See Richard Dawkins, *The God Delusion* (Boston: Houghton Mifflin,
      2006) and Daniel Dennett, *Breaking the Spell: Religion as a Natural Phe-
      nomenon* (New York: Viking, 2006).

[19] A new classic in this field is Ian Barbour, *Religion and Science: Historical and Contemporary Issues*, rev. ed. (London: SCM Press, 1998).

[20] The now foundational account is Pascale Boyer, *Religion Explained: The Evolutionary Origins of Religious Thought* (New York: Basic Books, 2001). Also see Dennett, *Breaking the Spell*; E. Thomas Lawson and Robert N. McCauley, *Bringing Ritual to Mind: Psychological Foundations of Cultural Forms* (Cambridge: Cambridge University Press, 2002) and Robert A. Hinde, *Why Gods Persist* (London and New York: Routledge, 1999).

[21] See Roger S. Gottlieb, *This Sacred Earth: Religion, Nature, Environment* (London and New York: Routledge, 1996) and *The Oxford Handbook of Religion and Ecology*, ed. Roger S. Gottlieb (New York: Oxford University Press, 2006).

[22] For contemporary studies of religion and the aesthetic, particularly the visual, see David Morgan, *The Sacred Gaze: Religious Visual Culture in Theory and Practice* (Berkeley, Los Angeles, and London: University of California Press, 2005) and *Religion, Art, and Visual Culture: A Cross-Cultural Reader*, ed. S. Brent Plate (New York and Hampshire, UK: Palgrave, 2002).

[23] See, for example, *Religion and Popular Culture in America*, ed. Bruce David Forbes and Jeffrey H. Mahan (Berkeley, Los Angeles, and London: University of California Press, 2005).

[24] For a fascinating survey of religion in cyberspace, consult *Religion Online: Finding Faith on the Internet*, ed. Lorne L. Dawson and Douglas E. Cowan (London and New York: Routledge, 2004).

[25] William James, *The Varieties of Religious Experience: A Study in Human Nature* (New York: Penguin Books, 1982), 35.

Additional reading

The following list of resources is designed to invite you to keep going after reading this book. It contains *General Reference* works in religion, classic and contemporary texts in religious-studies *Theory and Method*, and accessible treatments of a wide range of religious traditions, including *Buddhism, Chinese Religions, Christianity, Indigenous and Ancient Religions, Islam, Japanese Religions, Judaism, Religion in America, South Asian Religions*, and *Zoroastrianism*. This list is necessarily partial and selective, but it allows the study of religion to go wherever *you* want to take it next!

General reference

Bowker, John. *The Concise Oxford Dictionary of World Religions*. New York: Oxford University Press, 2000.

Eliade, Mircea. *The Encyclopedia of Religion*. 2nd ed. Woodbridge, CT: Macmillan Reference, 2004.

Esposito, John L., Darrell J. Fasching, and Todd Lewis. *World Religions Today*. New York: Oxford University Press, 2005.

Hinnells, John R. *The Penguin Dictionary of Religions*. New York: Penguin Books, 1997.

Hinnells, John R. *The Routledge Companion to the Study of Religion*. London and New York: Routledge, 2005.

Levinson, David. *Religion: A Cross-cultural Encyclopedia*. New York: Oxford University Press, 1998.

Melton, J. Gordon and Martin Baumann. *Religions of the World: A Comprehensive Encyclopedia of Beliefs and Practices*. Santa Barbara, CA: ABC-Clio Inc., 2002.

Sharma, Arvind. *Our Religions: The Seven World Religions Introduced by Preeminent Scholars from Each Tradition*. New York: HarperSan-Francisco, 1994.

Smart, Ninian. *The World's Religions*. 2nd ed. Cambridge: Cambridge University Press, 1998.

Smith, Huston. *The World's Religions: Our Great Wisdom Traditions*. Rev. ed. New York: HarperSanFrancisco, 1991.

Smith, Jonathan Z., ed. *The HarperCollins Dictionary of Religion*. New York: HarperSanFrancisco, 1995.

Theory and method

Berger, Peter L. *The Sacred Canopy: Elements of a Sociological Theory of Religion*. New York: Anchor Books, 1990.

Campbell, Joseph and Bill Moyers. *The Power of Myth*. New York: Anchor Books, 1991.

Capps, Walter H. *Religious Studies: The Making of a Discipline*. Minneapolis, MN: Augsburg Fortress Publishers, 1995.

Christ, Carol and Judith Plaskow, eds. *Womanspirit Rising: A Feminist Reader in Religion*. New York: HarperSanFrancisco, 1992.

Dennett, Daniel. *Breaking the Spell: Religion as a Natural Phenomenon*. New York: Penguin, 2007.

Douglas, Mary. *Purity and Danger: An Analysis of the Concepts of Pollution and Taboo*. London and New York: Routledge, 2002.

Durkheim, Emile. *The Elementary Forms of Religious Life*. Translated by Carol Cosman. New York: Oxford University Press, 2001.

Eliade, Mircea. *The Sacred and the Profane: The Nature of Religion*. USA: Harvest Books, 1968.

Eliade, Mircea. *Patterns in Comparative Religion*. Translated by Rosemary Sheed. Lincoln: University of Nebraska Press, 1996.

Freud, Sigmund. *The Future of an Illusion*. New York: W.W. Norton & Company, 1989.

Geertz, Clifford. *The Interpretation of Cultures*. New York: Basic Books, 2000.

Grimes, Ronald, ed. *Readings in Ritual Studies*. Upper Saddle River, NJ: Prentice Hall, 1996.

James, William. *Varieties of Religious Experience*. London and New York: Routledge, 2002.

Jung, Carl. G. *The Archetypes and the Collective Unconscious*. Translated by R.F.C. Hull. London: Routledge, 1991.

Jung, Carl. G. *Man and His Symbols*. Dayton, OH: Laurel Press, 1997.

Newberg, Andrew, Eugene d'Aquili, and Vince Rause. *Why God Won't Go Away: Brain Science and the Biology of Belief*. New York: Ballantine Books, 2002.

Otto, Rudolf. *The Idea of the Holy*. Translated by John W. Harvey. New York: Oxford University Press, 1958.

Paden, William E. *Interpreting the Sacred: Ways of Viewing Religion*. Boston: Beacon Press, 2003.

Pals, Daniel L. *Eight Theories of Religion*. 2nd ed. New York: Oxford University Press, 2006.

Patton, Kimberley C. and Benjamin C. Ray, eds. *A Magic Still Dwells: Comparative Religion in the Postmodern Age*. Berkeley: University of California Press, 2000.

Prentiss, Craig. R., ed. *Religion and the Creation of Race and Ethnicity*. New York: New York University Press, 2003.

Smith, Huston. *Why Religion Matters: The Fate of the Human Spirit in an Age of Disbelief*. New York: HarperSanFrancisco, 2001.

Smith, Jonathan Z. *Relating Religion: Essays in the Study of Religion*. Chicago: University of Chicago Press, 2004.

Smith, Wilfred Cantwell. *The Meaning and End of Religion*. Minneapolis, MN: Augsburg Fortress Publishers, 1991.

Tillich, Paul. *Dynamics of Faith*. London: HarperCollins Publishers, 2001.

Tillich, Paul. *Theology of Culture*. New York: Oxford University Press, 1964.

Turner, Victor. *The Ritual Process: Structure and Anti-Structure*. Piscataway, NJ: Aldine Transaction, 1995.

Van Gennep, Arnold. *The Rites of Passage*. London: Routledge, 2004.

Weber, Max. *The Protestant Ethic and the Spirit of Capitalism*. Translated by Stephen Kalberg. Oxford: Blackwell Publishing Limited, 2002.

Buddhism

Eckel, Malcolm David. *Buddhism: Origins, Beliefs, Practices, Holy Texts, Sacred Place*. New York: Oxford University Press, 2002.

Gethin, Rupert. *The Foundations of Buddhism*. New York: Oxford University Press, 1998.

Harvey, Peter. *An Introduction to Buddhism: Teachings, History and Practices*. Cambridge: Cambridge University Press, 1990.

Keown, Damien. *Buddhism: A Very Short Introduction*. New York: Oxford University Press, 2000.

Paul, Diana Y. *Women in Buddhism: Images of the Feminine in the Mahayana Tradition*. 2nd edn. Berkeley: University of California Press, 1985.

Rahula, Walpola. *What the Buddha Taught*. New York: Grove Press, 1974.

Robinson, Richard H., Willard L. Johnson, and Thanisarro Bhikkhu. *Buddhist Religions: A Historical Introduction*. 5th edn. Belmont, CA: Wadsworth Publishing, 2004.

Smith, Huston and Philip Novak. *Buddhism: A Concise Introduction*. San Francisco: HarperSanFrancisco, 2004.

Suzuki, Daisetz Teitaro. *An Introduction to Zen Buddhism*. New York: Grove Press, 1991.

Chinese religions (Confucianism and Daoism)

Ching, Julia. *Chinese Religions*. Maryknoll, NY: Orbis Books, 1993.

Kohn, Livia. *Daoism and Chinese Culture*. Honolulu: University of Hawaii Press, 2005.

Miller, James. *Daoism: A Short Introduction*. Oxford: Oneworld Publications, 2003.

Overmyer, Daniel L. *Religions of China: The World as a Living System*. Rev. ed. Long Grove, IL: Waveland Press, 1998.

Van Norden, Brian W., ed. *Confucius and the Analects: New Essays*. New York: Oxford University Press, 2003.

Christianity

Barrett, David B., George Thomas Kurian, and Todd M. Johnson, eds. *World Christian Encyclopedia*. 2nd ed. New York: Oxford University Press, 2001.

Crossan, John D. *The Historical Jesus: The Life of a Mediterranean Jewish Peasant*. New York: HarperCollins, 1993.

Ehrman, Bart. D. *The New Testament: A Historical Introduction to the Early Christian Writings*. New York: Oxford University Press, 2003.

Fredriksen, Paula. *From Jesus to Christ: The Origins of the New Testament Images of Christ*. 2nd ed. New Haven: Yale University Press, 2000.

Johnson, Luke. *The Real Jesus: The Misguided Quest for the Historical Jesus*. New York: HarperCollins, 1997.

Lindberg, Carter, ed. *The Reformation Theologians: An Introduction to Theology in the Early Modern Period*. Oxford: Blackwell, 2001.

McManners, John. *The Oxford Illustrated History of Christianity*. New York: Oxford University Press, 2001.

Neill, Stephen and Owen Chadwick. *A History of Christian Missions*. 2nd ed. London: Penguin, 1991.

Niebuhr, H. Richard. *Christ and Culture*. London: Harper Perennial, 1956.

Pagels, Elaine. *The Gnostic Gospels: A Startling Account of the Meaning of Jesus and the Origin of Christianity Based on Gnostic Gospels and Other Secret Texts*. New York: Vintage Books, 1989.

Sanders, E.P. *The Historical Figure of Jesus*. London: Penguin, 1996.

Southern, R.W. *Western Society and the Church in the Middle Ages*. London: Penguin, 1990.

Ware, Timothy. *The Orthodox Church*. 2nd edn. London: Penguin, 1993.

Woodhead, Linda. *Christianity: A Very Short Introduction*. New York: Oxford University Press, 2005.

Wuthnow, Robert. *Christianity in the 21st Century: Reflections on the Challenges Ahead*. New York: Oxford University Press, 2003.

Indigenous and ancient religions

Bottero, Jean. *Religion in Ancient Mesopotamia*. Translated by Teresa Lavender Fagan. Chicago: University of Chicago Press, 2004.

Eliade, Mircea. *Shamanism*. Translated by Willard R. Trask. Princeton: Princeton University Press, 2004.

Evans-Pritchard, Edward. *Nuer Religion*. New York: Oxford University Press. 1971.

Gill, Sam. *Native American Religions: An Introduction*. 2nd ed. Belmont, CA: Wadsworth Publishing, 2004.

Hackett, Rosalind. *Art and Religion in Africa*. London: Cassell, 1999.

Lewis, I.M. *Ecstatic Religion*. 3rd ed. London: Routledge, 2003.

Magesa, Laurent. *African Religion: The Moral Traditions of Abundant Life*. Maryknoll, NY: Orbis Books, 1997.

Martin, Joel W. *The Land Looks After Us: A History of Native American Religion*. New York: Oxford University Press, 2001.

Mbiti, John. *African Religions and Philosophy*. 2nd ed. Oxford: Heinemann, 1992.

Myerhoff, Barbara G. *Peyote Hunt: The Sacred Journey of the Huichol Indians*. Ithaca: Cornell University Press, 1976.

Ray, Benjamin C. *African Religions: Symbol, Ritual, and Community*. 2nd ed. Belmont, CA: Prentice Hall, 1999.

Shafer, Byron E., John R. Baines, David Silverman, and Leonard H. Lesko. *Religion in Ancient Egypt: Gods, Myth, and Personal Practice*. Ithaca: Cornell University Press, 1991.

Sullivan, Lawrence, ed. *Native Religions and Cultures of North America: Anthropology of the Sacred*. London: Continuum, 2003.

Swain, Tony and Garry Trompf. *The Religions of Oceania*. London and New York: Routledge, 1995.

Tripolitis, Antonia. *Religions of the Hellenistic-Roman Age*. Grand Rapids, MI: Wm. B. Eerdmans Publishing Company, 2001.

Turnbull, Colin. *The Forest People*. New York: Touchstone, 1961.

Vernant, Jean-Pierre. *Mortals and Immortals: Collected Essays*. Princeton: Princeton University Press, 1991.

Islam

Armstrong, Karen. *Muhammad: A Biography of the Prophet*. New York: HarperCollins, 1993.

Denny, Frederick. *An Introduction to Islam*. 3rd ed. Belmont, CA: Prentice Hall, 2005.

Esposito, John L. *What Everyone Needs to Know about Islam*. New York: Oxford University Press, 2002.

Esposito, John L. *Islam: The Straight Path*. New York: Oxford University Press, 2004.

Momen, Moojan. *An Introduction to Shi'i Islam: The History and Doctrines of Twelver Shi'ism*. New Haven: Yale University Press, 1987.

Nasr, Seyyed Hossein. *Islam: Religion, History, and Civilization*. New York: HarperSanFrancisco, 2002.

Ruthven, Malise. *Islam: A Very Short Introduction*. New York: Oxford University Press, 2000.

Schimmel, Annemarie. *Mystical Dimensions of Islam*. Chapel Hill: University of North Carolina Press, 1978.

Wolfe, Michael. *The Hadj: An American's Pilgrimage to Mecca*. New York: Grove Atlantic, 1998.

Japanese religions

Earhart, H. Byron. *Religion in the Japanese Experience: Sources and Interpretations*. 2nd ed. Belmont, CA: Wadsworth Publishing, 1996.

Earhart, H. Byron. *Japanese Religion: Unity and Diversity*. 4th ed. Belmont, CA: Wadsworth Publishing, 2003.

Ellwood, Robert S. and Richard Pilgrim. *Japanese Religion: A Cultural Perspective*. Belmont, CA: Prentice Hall, 1984.

Kasulis, Thomas P. *Shinto: The Way Home*. Honolulu: University of Hawaii Press, 2004.

Kitagawa, Joseph. *On Understanding Japanese Religion*. Princeton: Princeton University Press, 1987.

Judaism

de Lange, Nicholas. *An Introduction to Judaism*. Cambridge: Cambridge University Press, 2004.

Fishbane, Michael. *Judaism: Revelation and Traditions*. New York: HarperCollins, 1987.

Friedman, Richard E. *Who Wrote the Bible?* New York: HarperCollins, 1997.

Heschel, Abraham Joshua. *The Sabbath*. New York: Farrar, Straus and Giroux, 2005.

Holtz, Barry W. *Back to the Sources: Reading the Classic Jewish Texts*. New York: Simon and Schuster, 1986.

Jaffee, Martin. *Early Judaism*. Belmont, CA: Prentice Hall, 1996.

Neusner, Jacob. *Judaism: An Introduction*. London: Penguin, 2003.

Scholem, Gershom. *Major Trends in Jewish Mysticism*. New York: Schocken Books, 1995.

Solomon, Norman. *Judaism: A Very Short Introduction.* New York: Oxford University Press, 2000.
Wouk, Herman. *This Is My God.* Boston: Back Bay Books, 1992.

Religion in America

Ahlstrom, Sydney E. *A Religious History of the American People.* 2nd ed. New Haven: Yale University Press, 2004.
Albanese, Catherine L. *Nature Religion in America: From the Algonkian Indians to the New Age.* Chicago: University of Chicago Press, 1991.
Chidester, David. *Salvation and Suicide: An Interpretation of Jim Jones, the Peoples Temple, and Jonestown.* Bloomington: Indiana University Press, 2003.
Cox, Harvey. *Fire from Heaven: The Rise of Pentecostal Spirituality and the Reshaping of Religion in the Twenty-First Century.* Cambridge, MA: Da Capo Press, 2001.
Dawson, Lorne L. *Comprehending Cults: The Sociology of New Religious Movements.* 2nd ed. New York: Oxford University Press, 2006.
Eck, Diana. *On Common Ground: World Religions in America.* 2nd CD-ROM ed. New York: Columbia University Press, 2001.
Evans, Christopher Hodge and William R. Herzog, eds. *The Faith of 50 Million: Baseball, Religion, and American Culture.* Louisville, KY: Westminster John Knox Press, 2002.
Hackett, David, ed. *Religion and American Culture: A Reader.* 2nd ed. London and New York: Routledge, 2003.
Haddad, Yvonne. *The Muslims of America.* New York: Oxford University Press, 1991.
Hexham, Irving and Karla O. Poewe. *New Religions as Global Cultures: The Sacralization of the Human.* Boulder, CO: Westview Press, 2001.
McCarthy Brown, Karen. *Mama Lola: A Vodou Priestess in Brooklyn.* Berkeley: University of California Press, 2001.
McCloud, Aminah Beverly. *African American Islam.* London and New York: Routledge, 1994.
Melton, J. Gordon. *Encyclopedic Handbook of Cults in America.* London and New York: Routledge, 1992.
Prothero, Stephen. *American Jesus: How the Son of God Became a National Icon.* New York: Farrar, Straus and Giroux, 2003.
Raboteau, Albert J. *Afro-American Religious History: A Documentary Witness.* Durham, NC: Duke University Press, 1985.
Tabor, James. D. and Eugene V. Gallagher. *Why Waco? Cults and the Battle for Religious Freedom in America.* Berkeley: University of California Press, 1997.

Tweed, Thomas A., ed. *Retelling U.S. Religious History.* Berkeley: University of California Press, 1997.

Williams, Raymond. *Religions of Immigrants from India and Pakistan: New Threads in the American Tapestry.* Cambridge: Cambridge University Press, 1998.

Wuthnow, Robert. *America and the Challenges of Religious Diversity.* Princeton: Princeton University Press, 2005

South Asian religions (Hinduism, Sikhism, Jainism)

Dundas, Paul. *The Jains.* 2nd ed. London and New York: Routledge, 2002.

Eck, Diana. *Darsan: Seeing the Divine Image in India.* 3rd ed. New York: Columbia University Press, 1996.

Flood, Gavin. *An Introduction to Hinduism.* Cambridge: Cambridge University Press, 1996.

Fuller, C.J. *The Camphor Flame: Popular Hinduism and Society in India.* Princeton: Princeton University Press, 2004.

Huyler, Stephen. P. and Thomas Moore. *Meeting God: Elements of Hindu Devotion.* New Haven: Yale University Press, 2002.

Kalsi, Sewa Singh. *Simple Guide to Sikhism.* Folkstone, UK: Global Books Ltd, 1999.

Knipe, David. *Hinduism: Experiments in the Sacred.* Long Grove, IL: Waveland Press, 1998.

Knott, Kim. *Hinduism: A Very Short Introduction.* New York: Oxford University Press, 2000.

Mann, Gurinder Singh. *Sikhism.* Upper Saddle River, NJ: Prentice Hall, 2003.

Nesbitt, Eleanor. *Sikhism: A Very Short Introduction.* New York: Oxford University Press, 2005.

Zoroastrianism

Boyce, Mary. *Zoroastrians: Their Religious Beliefs and Practices.* 2nd ed. London and New York: Routledge, 2001.

Index

continuum

Related Titles

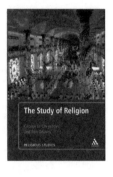

ISBN	TITLE	AUTHOR
978-08264-8046-0	Key Words in Buddhism	Geaves, Ron
978-08264-8047-7	Key Words in Christianity	Geaves, Ron
978-08264-8048-4	Key Words in Hinduism	Geaves, Ron
978-08264-8049-1	Key Words in Islam	Geaves, Ron
978-08264-8051-4	Key Words in Judaism	Geaves, Ron
978-08264-8050-7	Key Words in Religious Studies	Geaves, Ron
978-08264-9843-4	The Next Step in Studying Religion	Courville, Mathieu E.
978-08264-6449-1	The Study of Religion	Chryssides, George D.
		Geaves, Ron